THE COMPLETE
KIDS'
COOKBOOK

THE COMPLETE
KIDS'
COOKBOOK

All recipes in this book can be made by a child with little or no help from an adult. All the microwave recipes have been tested in a 600-700 watt microwave. Each recipe is set out to make cooking simple.

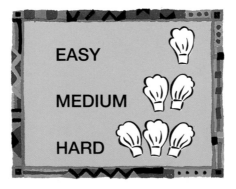

EASY

MEDIUM

HARD

Recipes are graded to help you learn. If you are just starting out to cook you might prefer to try the recipes marked easy (one chef's hat); when you have a little experience, try medium (two chefs' hats) and when you are more experienced try the harder recipes marked by three chefs' hats.

CONTENTS

GETTING STARTED 6

COOKING TERMS 8

MEASURING 9

HOW TO MICROWAVE 10

CHAPTER ONE
SNACKS AND DRINKS 12

CHAPTER TWO
PASTA AND PIZZA 42

CHAPTER THREE
CHICKEN, MEAT AND SEAFOOD 58

CHAPTER FOUR
MICROWAVE 90

CHAPTER FIVE
VEGETABLES AND SALADS 120

CHAPTER SIX
DESSERTS AND CAKES 142

CHAPTER SEVEN
SLICES, COOKIES AND GIFTS 176

INDEX 204

USEFUL INFORMATION 207

GETTING STARTED

Cooking is great fun and we've made it easy with our step-by-step recipes. Before you start, take time to get organised. Choose your recipe and read it all the way through, then check that you have all the ingredients. Collect everything you are going to use — all the ingredients and all the equipment.

If your recipe calls for chopped or shredded ingredients, do this before you begin. Also, open any cans and wash any vegetables or fruit. Grease any baking tins or microwave cookware if you need to.

If you need to use the oven for baking, turn it on to the correct temperature before you start the recipe. Arrange the oven shelves at the height you want before turning the oven on.

Before you start cooking in the microwave, read over our microwave section on page 11 to learn about the special methods and equipment that you need to know to make every recipe a success.

All the recipes are set out with step-by-step pictures so they are very easy to follow. Remember to finish each step before beginning the next one.

When you have finished cooking, clean up the kitchen. Put away all the ingredients and the equipment you have used. Wash the dishes — start with washing the least dirty dishes and then work up to the really messy pans. Dry dishes and put them back in their place. Wipe down your work surface with a clean cloth and then, I'm sure, you'll be allowed to cook again another day.

IMPORTANT SAFETY RULES

Here are a few hints and tips to make cooking safe and enjoyable.

✔ Always ask an adult for permission before you start.

✔ Before starting to cook, wash your hands well with soap and water. Wear an apron to protect your clothes and wear closed-in, non-slippery shoes to protect your feet.

✔ Unless you are allowed to use knives, ask an adult to help you chop things. Never cut directly on a kitchen bench or table — always use a chopping board. Pick knives up by the handle, not the blade. Keep fingers well clear when chopping foods.

✔ Take care when washing knives, too. Keep the sharp edge of the blade away from you and store the knives out of reach of any younger brothers or sisters.

✔ Always use oven mitts to remove anything from the oven or microwave. Also remember that anything you take from the top of the stove or the oven will stay hot for a while.

✔ Be very careful with pots and pans on the stove. Never reach across a hot saucepan — steam is very hot and can cause a nasty scald.

✔ Turn saucepan handles to the side when cooking so you don't knock them. Hold the handles of saucepans when stirring foods on the stove so that the pan won't slip. Use a wooden spoon — metal spoons can get hot when stirring hot foods.

✔ Place hot saucepans and ovenproof dishes on a chopping board when you take them from the oven or the stove. Never set a hot pan directly on the kitchen bench or table, unless it is covered with ceramic tiles.

✔ Don't put your fingers into hot pans or mixtures.

✔ Never use electrical appliances near water. Always have dry hands before you start to use any appliance.

✔ Remember to turn off the oven, the hotplate or gas ring or any other appliance when you have finished using it.

FIRST AID BURNS AND SCALDS

If you should burn or scald yourself, cool down the burn with cold water for 10 minutes (hold it under the cold tap). Protect against infection by gently covering the burn or scald with a clean, non-sticking bandage. Do not touch the burn.

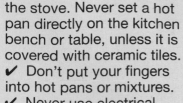

COOK'S TOOLS

The recipes in this book use the basic equipment found in most kitchens. If in doubt about any equipment you may need, ask an adult for some help.

There are many tools used in the kitchen to make cooking easy. There are wooden and metal spoons to stir with, spatulas to combine ingredients, bowls of varying sizes to mix things in, strainers or colanders to drain and rinse foods in, and a whole array of saucepans and baking trays to cook things in. There are wire racks for cooling cakes and cookies, metal spatulas to help you measure and also to spread toppings evenly over food.

COOKING TERMS

SOME COOKING TERMS

BEAT: To stir foods with a spoon or electric mixer until they are smooth.

BOILING POINT: When a liquid bubbles in a steady pattern and the bubbles break on the surface. Steam also starts to rise from the pan.

CHOP: Cut food carefully into small pieces. To chop finely is to cut foods as small as you can.

DRAIN: To strain away unwanted liquid from rice, pasta or vegetables using a colander or strainer. Do this over the kitchen sink so that water can drain away down the sink. OR fried foods need to be drained sometimes. Lift food out of frypan and place on brown paper or paper towels to absorb the extra oil or fat.

GRATE: To rub food against a grater. Do this over absorbent paper. Hold the grater with one hand and rub the food back and forth over the grating holes. This gives you long, thin pieces. For finely grated food, use the smallest holes.

GREASE: To rub baking tins and cooking utensils with butter, margarine or oil to stop foods sticking when you bake them.

KNEAD: Lightly rub and roll foods like pastry or scone dough on a floured surface until smooth and pliable.

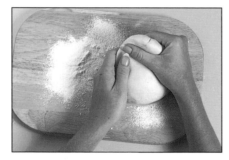

MASH: To squash cooked or very ripe foods with a fork or potato masher to make a soft mixture.

SEPARATING EGGS: When egg whites or yolks are needed for a recipe. Hold the egg over a small plate and carefully crack the shell with a knife. Let the egg fall out onto the plate, place a small glass over the yolk and then carefully tip the white into a bowl. If any yolk gets into the white, you can easily remove it with a piece of eggshell.

SIMMER: To cook food over a very low heat, so that only a few bubbles appear over the surface. When a recipe calls for food to boil and then simmer, simply turn the heat down to the lowest setting.

SLICE: To cut foods such as apples, carrots or tomatoes into thin rounds or sections.

WHISK: To mix ingredients together with a balloon-shaped, wire mixer (a whisk) by moving in a circular motion until smooth or combined.

MEASURING

MEASURING UP

Careful measuring of ingredients makes for a successful recipe. You will need a set of dry measuring cups, which usually come in a set of four: 1 cup, ½ cup, ⅓ cup and ¼ cup measures. These are used to measure ingredients such as flour and sugar. You will also need a liquid measuring cup that usually has a lip for easy pouring and lines on the side that mark the different liquid measures. Milk, cream, water and juice are measured with this cup. Measuring spoons will also be needed to measure small amounts. They are marked and measure 1 tablespoon, 1 teaspoon, ½ teaspoon and ¼ teaspoon.

DRY MEASURES

Take care to use the correct size measuring cup as stated in the recipe, especially if you are baking cakes or cookies. Spoon the dry ingredients lightly into the measuring cup and level it off with a spatula. It's a good idea to do this over a piece of absorbent paper to avoid any mess.

In some recipes you will need to do some simple maths to get the correct amount you need. For example, you may need ⅔ cup flour for a recipe, so simply measure out ⅓ cup using the correct measure and then another ⅓ cup and add both to the recipe.

LIQUID MEASURES

To measure a liquid place the measuring cup on the bench or board, add some of the liquid and bend down so that your eyes are level with the measurement marks. Check to see if you have enough liquid; if necessary, pour in more. If you have too much, simply pour out the extra.

SPOON MEASURES

Measuring spoons are different from the spoons you use for eating. They are used to measure small amounts.

To measure liquids, choose the correct size spoon for the amount you need and carefully pour the liquid into the spoon.

BUTTER

Butter is generally measured in grams. You will find that blocks of butter have a weight marking on the side of the wrapper. Use a small knife to cut through the butter at the correct marking and then unwrap it. Butter can also be weighed using a kitchen scale.

It's a good idea to hold the spoon over a cup or jug to avoid spills.

To measure dry ingredients, fill the correct size spoon with dry ingredients and then carefully level off the top with a metal spatula.

HOW TO MICROWAVE

MICROWAVE KNOW HOW

Microwave cooking is great fun, too. Before you start, read this page to learn the special techniques and equipment you need to make your recipes a success.

All microwave ovens are different. Before beginning to cook get to know a little about your microwave oven. You may need to ask an adult to help you.

- Firstly, find out what wattage your microwave oven is — this is important to determine cooking times. All our recipes were tested in a 600-700 watt microwave. If yours has fewer watts, foods will take a little longer to cook.
- Learn how to operate or set your microwave oven from High to Low and how to set the timer.
- Here are the temperatures and percentages we used:

High: 100% power
Medium/High: 75% power
Medium: 50% power
Low: 30% power

- Some foods cook a little more quickly than others in a particular dish. These foods need stirring as they cook, so that they cook evenly.
- Place microwave dishes in the centre of the microwave oven.

MICROWAVE CONTAINERS

- Lots of special microwave containers are made out of plastic. Before you use them, look underneath the dish to make sure it tells you how it can be used. Some say they are suitable for most things but not for foods with lots of fat, oil or sugar. These get very, very, hot and if you're not using a suitable plastic dish, the heat could damage it or even make it melt!
- Don't use any metal containers in the microwave.
- Don't use any dishes, plates, mugs or cups that have a silver or gold trim. These metals react badly with microwaves. The nice trim could turn a nasty colour, or more important, it may cause sparks that could damage the oven.
- Don't use fine bone china, crystal bowls or glasses.
- Some pottery mugs or casserole dishes have a glaze that contains small amounts of metal. These can get very hot in the microwave and could give you a nasty burn — check with an adult before using if you're not sure.
- The best containers to use, especially for cooking with liquid, are those with a handle for safe removal from the microwave. Don't forget — the oven might feel cool, but the dish could be hot, so have some oven mitts ready.

MICROWAVE COOK'S TOOLS

Microwave cooking requires some specially-made equipment, because ordinary pans and dishes can damage the microwave. There are wooden and micro-safe spoons to stir with, racks to elevate dishes in the oven and micro-safe dishes to cook things in.

MICROWAVE SAFETY POINTS

✔ Always use oven mitts to remove anything from the microwave. Remember that anything you take from the microwave oven will be hot for a while.

✔ When you uncover foods just out of the microwave take great care that the steam doesn't burn you. Lift the far side of the cover up first, letting the steam go up and out away from you.

✔ When stirring microwave dishes, hold the container with oven mitts as you stir.

✔ Never operate the microwave oven without food inside.

✔ Never put anything made of metal into the microwave.

MICROWAVE COOKING TERMS

COVER: Make sure you do "cover" when the recipe tells you to or food might dry out. But also, don't forget to leave off the lid or cling wrap when the recipe says "cook uncovered". If you leave a cover on when it should not be, it could cause the food to boil over.

GREASE: To brush micro containers and cooking utensils with melted butter or oil to stop foods sticking.

PIERCE: This is when you make holes in the cling wrap cover in several places with a fork to avoid liquid boiling over.

RACKS: These are used for lifting dishes up a little from the bottom of the microwave oven. It helps cakes and some desserts to cook more evenly. If you don't have a rack, you can use a small, upturned saucer or dish.

STIR: We say this a lot when microwaving, because if you don't stir the food or liquid regularly, the outside of the food gets hot while the middle is only slightly warm.

CHAPTER ONE
SNACKS AND DRINKS

These tasty treats are perfect for those in-between times and make great after-school or weekend snacks. They are fun to make and serve to friends and family.

CHEESE TOAST

Serves 6

1 cup grated Cheddar
    cheese
2 tablespoons chutney
1 tablespoon grated onion
1 tablespoon tomato sauce
1 teaspoon Worcestershire
    sauce
25 g butter
6 thick slices wholegrain
    bread

1
Put the grated cheese into a mixing bowl.

2
Add chutney, onion, tomato sauce + Worcestershire sauce.

3
Melt butter in small pan. Stir in to mixing bowl.

4
Turn the grill on to high.

5
Toast the bread on one side only.

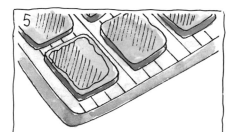

6
Spread cheese mixture on untoasted side.

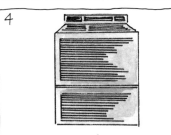

7
Put it back under grill until cheese is melted.

8
Slice and serve it straight away.

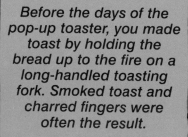

Before the days of the pop-up toaster, you made toast by holding the bread up to the fire on a long-handled toasting fork. Smoked toast and charred fingers were often the result.

CINNAMON TOAST 🍳

Serves 6

6 tablespoons caster sugar
2 tablespoons cinnamon
6 thick slices bread
softened butter

1. Put the sugar into a small jar or cup.

2. Add the cinnamon and stir until mixed.

3. Put the bread in toaster.

4. Toast it until golden.

5. Butter toast immediately.

6. Sprinkle cinnamon and sugar evenly over.

7. Slice the toast + serve.

8. Put lid on jar and use any leftover cinnamon + sugar any time.

GARLIC TOAST

Serves 4

25 g butter
½ teaspoon garlic salt
6 thin slices wholegrain
  bread

1. Turn oven to 150°C (300°F)

2. LOW HEAT
Melt the butter.

3. Mix in the garlic.

4. Brush it on each piece of bread.

5. Cut each piece of bread into 3 strips.

6. Put (butter side up) on to an oven sheet.

7. Bake for 30 minutes.

8. Serve hot with soup.

ONION DIP

Serves 6–8

1 x 45 g packet of dried
   French onion-style soup
2 tablespoons vinegar
¾ cup softened cream
   cheese
1 cup plain yoghurt
¼ cup chopped parsley

1
Empty packet of soup into small bowl.

2
Add vinegar. Stir it a little.

3
Put it aside for about 30 minutes.

4
Stir in cream cheese.

5
Stir in the yoghurt stirring it all well.

6
Stir in the parsley. Put a lid on bowl.

7
Put in fridge until needed.

8
Put on a serving plate with crackers or chips.

TASTY TUNA TRIANGLES

Makes 12 triangles

170 g can sandwich tuna
130 g can creamed corn
1 tablespoon chopped
   parsley leaves
1 egg
6 slices white bread
⅓ cup oil

1
Pour tuna and corn into a mixing bowl.

2
Add the chopped parsley and egg. Mix well.

3
Cut crusts off bread.

4
Spread mixture on bread slices.

5
Cut slices into triangles.

6
Heat the oil in a fry pan. When it's hot, put in a few triangles.

7
When they are golden lift out with a spatula and put on paper to drain.

8
Cook the rest of the triangles and drain on paper.

NACHOS

Serves 2

½ cup three bean mix
2 cups corn chips
¼ cup taco sauce
¼ cup chopped avocado
⅓ cup grated mozzarella
  cheese
1 tablespoon sour cream

1
Turn oven to 180°C (350°F).

2

Put beans in a bowl. Mash with a fork.

3

Spoon beans into the centre of 2 ovenproof dishes.

4
Arrange corn chips around the beans.

5

Pour taco sauce on the beans.

6

Put avocado on top of sauce.

7

Sprinkle the grated cheese over.

8

Bake for 10 minutes. Serve topped with a spoonful of sour cream.

HOT BEAN DOGS

Makes 4

4 continental frankfurts
4 hot dog rolls
120 g butter
225 g can baked beans
 in tomato sauce
4 tablespoons coarsely
 grated Cheddar cheese
4 tablespoons sweet
 mustard

Cut 5 slits into each frankfurt.

Cut 5 more slits across the first to make a pattern.

3. Put franks under hot grill. When one side is brown, turn and cook the other side.

4. Split rolls in half and spread with butter.

5. Put rolls on plates. Spoon baked beans on rolls.

6. Sprinkle with cheese.

7. Put hot frankfurt on top of cheese. (Use tongs.)

8. Top with a spoon of mustard and serve.

SAVOURY PUFF PINWHEELS 👨‍🍳👨‍🍳

Makes about 12

1 sheet ready-rolled
   puff pastry
⅓ cup cream cheese
   spread
2 tablespoons tomato
   sauce

½ teaspoon dried oregano
   leaves
60 g sliced salami

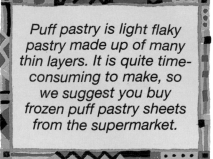

Puff pastry is light flaky pastry made up of many thin layers. It is quite time-consuming to make, so we suggest you buy frozen puff pastry sheets from the supermarket.

1 Put the sheet of pastry on a big chopping board.

2 Spread the cheese spread over the pastry.

3 Spread the tomato sauce over.

4 Sprinkle with the oregano and the salami slices.

5 Roll up the pastry into a tight roll. Wrap in plastic wrap.

6 Put roll in the fridge for 1 hour.

7 Take roll out. Cut into slices about 2cm wide. Turn oven to 200°C (400°F).

8 Bake for 15 minutes until crisp and golden.

PIZZA SNACKS 🧑‍🍳

Serves 4

2 hamburger buns
30 g butter, melted
¼ cup tomato sauce
12 thin slices of salami

8 thin slices of cheese
 (about 5 x 2 cm)
1 teaspoon dried oregano

1
Cut the hamburger buns in half.

2
Brush the 4 halves with melted butter.

3
Toast lightly under grill. Leave the grill on.

4
Brush toasted halves with tomato sauce.

5
Top each half with 3 slices of salami.

6
Put 2 slices of cheese on top of each.

7
Sprinkle a little oregano on top.

8
Put back under grill till cheese is bubbly.

SCHNITZEL SANDWICH

Makes 2
¼ cup oil
1 onion, sliced
2 Vienna schnitzels
4 thick slices bread,
   lightly toasted
2 eggs
2 tablespoons barbecue
   sauce
1 tomato, sliced

1. Heat half the oil in a big, heavy fry pan.

2. Fry onions until brown. Take out of pan, drain on absorbent paper. Keep warm.

3. Pour the rest of the oil into the fry pan.

4. Cook schnitzels for 2 minutes. Turn over and cook the other side for 2 minutes.

5. Put schnitzels on toast. Top with onions.

6. Fry eggs. Put the cooked eggs on top of the onions.

7. Pour on sauce and put tomato on top.

8. Top with toast and serve hot.

CHICKEN NOODLE OMELETTE 🐓🐓

Serves 2

2 cups water
85 g packet chicken-
    flavoured instant noodles
1 cup chopped, cooked
    chicken

2 teaspoons finely chopped
    parsley
2 eggs, lightly beaten
2 tablespoons grated
    Cheddar cheese

Omelettes are easy to make and good for you. You can add your favourite things; try chopped tomato and ham or salami. Bean sprouts and chopped celery give lots of crunch.

1
Boil the water in a small pan.

2
Add the noodles and flavour sachet to pan.

3
Cook noodles as directed. Drain well.

4
Put noodles, chicken, parsley and eggs in a bowl. Mix well.

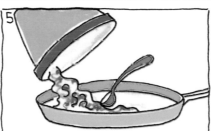
5
Put the mixture in a 20cm non-stick fry pan.

6
Cook for 5 minutes without stirring.

7
Sprinkle with the cheese.

Put under a hot grill. Cook for 2 minutes to brown. Serve hot.

SUNKEN SUBMARINES

Makes 4

2 long crusty bread rolls
2 tablespoons garlic butter
225 g can spaghetti in
   tomato and cheese
   sauce
2 thick slices devon or ham
2 slices processed cheese

1. Heat oven to 180°c (350°F). Lightly grease an oven tray.

2. Cut rolls in half and spread with butter.

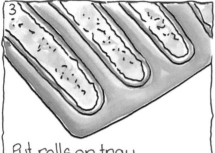

3. Put rolls on tray.

4. Spoon spaghetti onto each roll.

5. Chop devon and sprinkle over spaghetti.

6. Cut cheese into thin strips.

7. Arrange cheese strips on the devon.

8. Bake for 12 minutes. Serve hot.

CHICKEN POCKETS

Makes 3

3 oval pocket breads
3 tablespoons mayonnaise
3 large lettuce leaves
3 tablespoons corn relish
9 chicken nuggets

1 Carefully split pocket breads open.

2 Put bread on serving plates.

3 Spread mayonnaise on inside of bread.

4 Chop lettuce thinly.

5 Fill bread pockets with lettuce. Spoon relish over.

6 Grill chicken nuggets 3 minutes.

7 Turn nuggets; cook 3 minutes more.

8 Put cooked nuggets into pockets. Serve hot.

CHICKEN CLUB SANDWICH 🐔🐔🐔

Preparation time: 20 minutes
Total cooking time: 10 minutes
Makes 2

⭐

½ BBQ chicken
4 rashers bacon
¼ cup (60 g/2 oz) mayonnaise
1 tablespoon wholegrain
mustard
4 slices rye bread
½ avocado, thinly sliced
2 lettuce leaves, shredded
1 tomato, sliced

1 Remove the meat from the chicken bones (including the skin) and cut into shreds.

2 Fry the bacon until crisp and brown. Drain on paper towels.

3 Place the mayonnaise and mustard in a bowl and stir until well combined.

4 Toast the bread, and spread 2 slices with the mayonnaise mixture. Top with the avocado, lettuce and tomato.

5 Put the shredded chicken and bacon on next, and season with salt and pepper. Top with the other slices of toast, cut in half diagonally and serve.

B.L.T. 🐛🐛🐛

Preparation time: 15 minutes
Total cooking time: 5
minutes
Serves 2

★

4 rashers bacon
4 slices thick toasting bread
1 1/2 tablespoons mayonnaise
2 large lettuce leaves
1 small tomato

1 Cut the rind from the bacon and cut each rasher in half. Heat a frying pan and add the bacon; cook until crisp and brown. Drain on paper towels.

2 Toast the bread, and spread mayonnaise onto each slice.

3 Shred the lettuce finely, and slice the tomato.

4 Place the lettuce, tomato and bacon onto 2 of the toast slices; top with the other slices.

5 Cut the sandwiches into triangles and serve immediately.

HAM AND CHEESE PUFFS

Makes 2

1 sheet ready-rolled puff pastry
2 slices sandwich ham
2 slices tasty cheese

1. Turn oven to 180°c (350°F).

2. Put pastry on large cutting board. Cut into 4 squares.

3. Put the slices of ham on 2 pieces of pastry.

4. Top the ham with the cheese slices.

5. Put the plain pastry on top. Press edges together.

6. Trim around edges with a pastry wheel.

7. Put on a baking **tray**. Bake for 12 minutes.

8. Cut in half to serve.

STICKY BUNS

Makes 12

60 g butter
½ cup brown sugar } Step 1
2 tablespoons sultanas
2¼ cups plain flour
2 teaspoons baking powder
30 g butter (Step 3)

2 ripe bananas, mashed
½ cup milk
30 g butter, melted
2 tablespoons
  brown sugar } Step 6

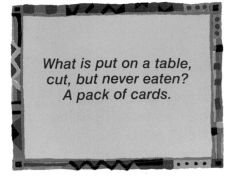

*What is put on a table,
cut, but never eaten?
A pack of cards.*

1 Turn oven to 190°C (375°F). Melt the 60 g butter + the ½ cup brown sugar in a pan.

2 Stir in sultanas. Spoon mixture into base of 12 deep muffin pans.

3 Sift flour + baking powder into bowl. Rub in the 30 g butter till it looks crumbly.

4 Add mashed bananas + milk. Mix it all quickly to form a soft dough.

5 Knead it. Roll out on floured surface till it's 20 x 15 cm.

6 Spread melted butter over. Sprinkle brown sugar over.

7 Firmly roll up (from long side). Cut neatly into 12 slices.

8 Put cut-side down in pans. Bake 12-15 minutes.

31

APPLE MUFFINS

Makes 12

1 small ripe banana
1 cup white self-raising
    flour
½ cup wholemeal
    self-raising flour
⅔ cup sugar
½ cup choc bits
1 egg, lightly beaten
⅔ cup milk
¼ cup oil

1 Turn oven to 180°c (350°F).	**2** Brush a 12-hole muffin pan with a little oil.	**3** Mash banana in a large bowl.
4 Sift flour into the bowl (add the husks left in the sifter).	**5** Put in sugar, choc bits, egg, milk and oil.	**6** Stir with a fork until well mixed.
7 Spoon mixture into muffin pan. Fill the holes ⅔ full.	*Yummy hot muffins make a great snack. Drink a glass of milk or soy milk with a Chocanana Muffin and you'll be absolutely bursting with energy.*	**8** Bake for 20 minutes or until golden. Turn onto a rack to cool.

CHOCANANA MUFFINS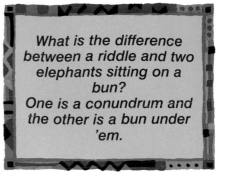

Makes about 12

1 cup wholemeal
   self-raising flour
½ cup brown sugar
½ cup oat bran
½ teaspoon cinnamon
¼ cup chopped pecans
2 large green apples

1 egg
⅔ cup milk
60 g butter, melted

What is the difference between a riddle and two elephants sitting on a bun?
One is a conundrum and the other is a bun under 'em.

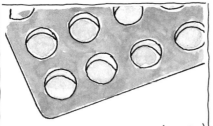

Turn oven to 220°C (425°F) Grease 12 muffin pans.

2 Sift flour into a bowl. Add sugar, oat bran, cinnamon + pecans.

3 Peel, then grate the apples. Stir them into the bowl.

4 Mix egg, milk and melted butter in a jug.

5 Add to bowl all at once. Stir with a fork.

6 Stir until just mixed. It is supposed to look lumpy.

7 Almost fill the pans with the batter.

8 Bake 15-20 minutes or until golden

Serve warm with butter + jam if you like

FRECKLE FACES 🎩🎩

Makes about 12

1 cup self-raising flour
2 tablespoons caster sugar
1 egg, lightly beaten
½ cup milk
1 teaspoon imitation vanilla
  essence
1 teaspoon oil
¼ cup soft cream cheese
¼ cup hazelnut spread
2 tablespoons hundreds
  and thousands

1 Sift flour and sugar into a mixing bowl.

2 Add the egg, milk and vanilla. Beat with a fork until smooth.

3 Brush a non-stick pan with the oil. Put on stove.

4 When pan is hot, put spoonfuls of mixture in about 4 cm apart.

5 Cook for 1 minute, turn, cook other side for 1 minute or until bottom is golden.

6 Leave to cool. Spread half of each pikelet with cheese.

7 Spread other half with hazelnut spread.

Pancake batter can be made one day before you need it. Store in a jug, covered with plastic wrap, in the refrigerator.

8 Sprinkle with hundreds and thousands.

FRUITY YOGHURT POPS

Makes 6

2 x 200 g cartons vanilla-
flavoured yoghurt
170 g can passionfruit pulp
in syrup
4 large strawberries
1 tablespoon icing sugar
ice choc magic or
2 tablespoons melted
chocolate

1. Put yoghurt and passionfruit in a mixing bowl.

2. Pull off green stems from strawberries.

3. Chop strawberries into small pieces. Put into bowl.

4. Add icing sugar to bowl. Mix well.

5. Spoon mixture into 6 ice-cream moulds or paper cups.

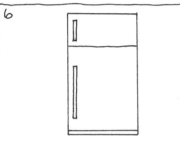
6. Put in freezer for 1 hour.

7. Press a wooden ice-cream stick in centre of each pop. Put back in freezer for 2 hours.

8. Turn pops out of mould or pull paper away. Drizzle with chocolate before eating.

SUPER SMOOTHIES AND SHAKES

Choc-mint Dream

Fruit Salad Smoothie

Smoothies and shakes are simple to make, look fantastic and are absolutely scrumptious to drink. They only take a minute to prepare and make a great snack or after-school treat. Some of these recipes are almost a meal in themselves! No time for breakfast? Whip up an energy shake!

Feel like some fruit? Try a smoothie loaded with fresh fruit. You'll be getting a taste treat and a vitamin-packed drink that will keep you going all day long.

Whizz these drinks up in your blender and serve them in a big, tall glass. Use your imagination and decorate with coloured sprinkles, little umbrellas, pieces of fruit or whatever you have on hand.

SMOOTHIE CHECKLIST

Collect all the things you will need to make your smoothie.

- Blender
- Ice-cream scoop; rubber or plastic spatula (for scraping mixture out of the blender)
- Ice cubes or ice-cream
- Fruit
- Cold milk
- Flavourings
- Decorations

CHERRY-BERRY SPIDER

Makes 2

4 cherries and 4 blueberries
2 tablespoons raspberry or blackcurrant cordial
2 cups lemonade
2 scoops vanilla ice-cream

1 Put two cherries and two blueberries in each glass.
2 Add 1 tablespoon cordial to each glass.
3 Gently pour on lemonade.
4 Top each glass with a scoop of ice-cream. Decorate with cherries and blueberries.
5 Serve immediately with a spoon and straw.

CHOC-MINT DREAM

Makes 2

4 scoops choc-mint ice-cream
1½ cups milk
chocolate sprinkles

1 Put 2 scoops of ice-cream and milk in blender.
2 Blend until smooth.
3 Pour into tall glasses.
4 Top each glass with a scoop of ice-cream and chocolate sprinkles.
5 Serve immediately with a spoon and straw.

Energy Shake

Melty Malted Smoothie

PINA COLADA SMOOTHIE

Makes 2

1½ cups pineapple juice
1 banana
½ cup canned thick coconut
   milk
½ cup ice cubes (optional)

1 Put all ingredients in blender.
2 Blend together until smooth.
3 Pour into tall glasses to
   serve.

MELTY MALTED SMOOTHIE

Makes 2

2 cups milk
2 tablespoons drinking
   chocolate
2 tablespoons malt powder
2 scoops vanilla ice-cream
1 flaked chocolate bar, cut in
   half
2 scoops vanilla ice-cream,
   extra

1 Put milk, chocolate, malt and
   2 scoops ice-cream in
   blender.
2 Blend together until smooth.
3 Pour into 2 big mugs, microwave on High 1 minute or
   until hot.
4 Pour into 2 mugs, top with a
   scoop of ice-cream and half
   a chocolate bar.
5 Serve immediately with a
   spoon.

FRUIT SALAD SMOOTHIE

Makes 2

1½ cups milk
2 scoops vanilla ice-cream
1 cup chopped fruit
   (passionfruit, strawberries,
   banana, etc)
½ cup ice-cubes
2 tablespoons honey

1 Put all ingredients in blender.
2 Blend together until smooth.
3 Pour into tall glasses to
   serve.

ENERGY SHAKE

Makes 2

1½ cups skim milk or
   soy milk
1 tablespoon skim milk
   powder
½ cup yoghurt
1 tablespoon honey
1 banana
6 strawberries (optional)
cinnamon, to sprinkle

1 Put all ingredients in blender.
2 Blend together until smooth.
3 Pour into tall glasses to
   serve.
4 Sprinkle a little cinnamon on
   top.

COFFEE FLOAT

Serves 6

2 tablespoons instant coffee
    powder
2 tablespoons sugar
¾ cup hot water
1 teaspoon vanilla essence
4 cups cold milk
6 scoops vanilla ice-cream
cocoa powder, to sprinkle

1
Dissolve coffee and sugar in the hot water.

2
Pour into a bowl. Add the vanilla essence and milk.

3
Stir it all well.

4
Chill in the fridge until it's very cold.

5
Whisk until it's foamy.

6
Put a scoop of ice-cream into 6 tall glasses.

7
Fill each glass with mixture.

8
Sprinkle with a little cocoa powder. Pop in a straw and serve.

BANANA MILKSHAKE

Serves 3

1½ cups milk
1 medium-sized banana
1 tablespoon honey
1 egg
2 tablespoons banana-
  flavoured yoghurt
2 scoops vanilla ice-cream
2 ice cubes

1. Pour milk into blender.

2. Peel the banana.

3. Chop up the banana. Add it to the blender.

4. Add the honey, egg and banana yoghurt.

5. Add ice cream + ice.

6. Put lid on blender. Blend well until smooth.

7. Pour it into 3 glasses.

8. Pop in straws + serve.

LEMON CORDIAL

Makes 1 litre

4 large lemons
4 cups sugar
2 cups water
2 teaspoons citric acid
1 teaspoon lemon essence

1 Squeeze juice from lemons (You'll get about 1 cup juice)

2 Put juice into a large saucepan. Add the sugar.

3 Add water + citric acid.

4 Bring it to the boil.

5 MEDIUM HEAT
Boil 10 minutes. BE CAREFUL IT DOESN'T BOIL OVER!

6 Set it aside to cool.

7 Stir in the lemon essence.

8 Pour into 2 sterilised bottles with lids.
Mix with lemonade or water to drink.

FRUIT PUNCH 🍴

Serves 10

1.25 L canned orange juice
425 g can fruit salad
1 orange
1 lemon
750 mL bottle of lemonade
 (chilled)

1. Pour the can of juice into a large bowl or jug.

2. Add the whole can of fruit salad.

3. Squeeze juice from orange

4. Pour it into bowl.

5. Squeeze juice from lemon Add it to bowl.

6. Put in the fridge until it's really cold.

7. Just before serving, add the lemonade.

8. Stir it and then serve it.

CHAPTER TWO

PASTA AND PIZZA

Two of Italy's special gifts to the world – pasta and pizza. Everybody loves them and they are so simple to make. To whip up a satisfying and scrumptious meal, simply choose your favourite recipe and add a crispy salad and a crunchy loaf of bread. Mmmm!

FABULOUS FETTUCCINE 👨‍🍳👨‍🍳👨‍🍳

Serves 4

375 g fettuccine
4 rashers bacon
220 g can mushrooms
   in butter sauce
130 g can creamed corn
2 medium zucchini
½ cup cream
3 spring onions, chopped
⅓ cup grated Parmesan
   cheese

1. Boil a big pot of water. Carefully add fettuccine.

2. Boil for 10 minutes. Drain well.

3. Chop bacon; throw away rinds. Fry gently.

4. Stir in mushrooms and corn.

5. Slice zucchini into rounds.

6. Add to pan with cream. Simmer for 5 minutes.

7. Add spring onions and Parmesan cheese. Stir.

Parmesan cheese is especially delicious if you grate it yourself rather than buying the already-grated stuff. It only takes a minute and you can buy whole pieces of Parmesan from the supermarket.

8. Add pasta to pan and mix well. Serve immediately.

44

SPAGHETTI BOLOGNESE 🍄🍄🍄

Serves 4

2 tablespoons olive oil
1 medium onion, finely
   chopped
500 g minced beef
500 ml bottled spaghetti
   sauce
2 tablespoons tomato
   paste
¼ cup red wine
2 beef stock cubes,
   crumbled
½ cup frozen peas, rinsed
   and drained
2 cloves garlic, crushed
1 tablespoon finely
   chopped parsley
500 g packet spaghetti

1 Heat oil in a big heavy pan.

2 Fry onions and mince. Stir until all red has gone.

3 Add sauce, tomato paste, wine and stock cubes. Bring to boil.

4 Add peas. Turn down heat and simmer for 10 minutes.

5 Stir in garlic and parsley

6 Boil a big pot of water. Carefully add spaghetti.

7 Boil spaghetti for 10 minutes. Drain well.

Always cook spaghetti in a large pot of boiling water. The water is boiling when bubbles rise up to the surface and steam rises out of the pot.

8 Put spaghetti in a big serving bowl. Pour sauce over and serve.

TUNA PASTA BAKE 👨‍🍳 👨‍🍳

Serves 4

250 g macaroni
130 g corn kernels, drained
1 cup frozen peas, rinsed
   and drained
180 g can tuna in brine,
   drained

1 cup milk
22 g packet white
   sauce mix
½ cup sour cream
½ cup crushed cheese-
   flavoured biscuits

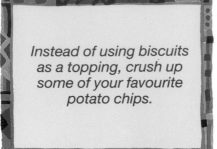

Instead of using biscuits as a topping, crush up some of your favourite potato chips.

1 Turn oven to 180°c (350°F).	2 Boil a big pot of water. Carefully add macaroni.	3 Boil macaroni for 10 minutes. Drain well.
4 Put macaroni, corn, peas and tuna in a big bowl.	5 Put milk and sauce mix in a small pan. Stir until it boils and thickens.	6 Pour sauce into the bowl. Add cream. Mix well.

7 Put in a shallow casserole. Sprinkle with biscuits.

8 Bake for 20 minutes, then serve.

CORNY CHICKEN CANNELLONI 🍳🍳🍳

Serves 4

250 g packet frozen
 chopped leaf spinach
1 small onion, finely chopped
30 g butter
250 g chicken mince
130 g can corn kernels,
 drained
130 g can diced capsicum,
 drained
2 tablespoons dried
 breadcrumbs
1 egg, lightly beaten
120 g packet instant
 cannelloni shells
250 ml bottled spaghetti
 sauce
140 g jar cream cheese
 spread

1. Gently cook spinach, onion and butter in a small pan for 10 minutes.

2. Pour into a bowl and leave to cool.

3. Put mince into pan and cook, stirring, for 3 minutes.

4. Mix into spinach with corn, capsicum, breadcrumbs and egg.

5. Turn oven to 180°c (350°F). Spoon mixture into shells.

6. Spread ¼ cup spaghetti sauce in a shallow casserole dish.

7. Arrange shells in dish. Pour remaining sauce over and dot with cheese.

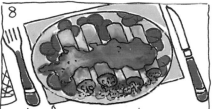

8. Bake for 40 minutes. Take out, leave 5 minutes, then serve.

Pasta is made from durum flour, a special type of "hard" flour, mixed with eggs and rolled out to make spaghetti, shells, spirals, tubes, tiny stars, cartwheels and many other shapes.

MACARONI CHEESE 👨‍🍳👨‍🍳

Serves 4

30 g butter
4 rashers bacon, cut
  in thin strips
2 tablespoons plain flour
2 cups milk
4 cups cooked macaroni

1 zucchini, finely chopped
1½ cups grated Cheddar
  cheese
1 tablespoon packaged
  breadcrumbs

1 Melt butter in a pan. Add bacon strips and cook 5 minutes.

2 Add flour and stir for 3 minutes.

3 Add milk a little at a time. Keep stirring.

4 Stir until sauce boils and is thick. Take pan off heat.

5 Add macaroni, zucchini and 1 cup cheese. Mix well.

6 Turn oven to 180°C (350°F). Spoon into a shallow ovenproof dish.

7 Sprinkle with the cheese and breadcrumbs.

Bake 25 minutes or until golden. Serve hot.

MACARONI MINCE 🍳🍳🍳

Serves 4

1 tablespoon oil
1 onion, finely chopped
500 g lean minced beef
sprinkle of salt and pepper
425 g can peeled tomatoes
¾ cup tomato purée

1 teaspoon dried oregano
¼ teaspoon sugar
1 cup water
1½ cups small shell
  macaroni

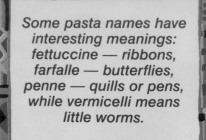

Some pasta names have interesting meanings: fettuccine — ribbons, farfalle — butterflies, penne — quills or pens, while vermicelli means little worms.

1
MEDIUM HEAT
Heat oil in a big pan. Fry onion until soft.

2
MEDIUM HEAT
Add mince. Cook, stirring till all red has gone.

3
Add salt, pepper, canned tomatoes, purée, oregano sugar and water.

4
MEDIUM HEAT
Stir it all together well until it starts to boil.

5
LOW HEAT
Turn heat to low and simmer for 40 minutes.

6
HIGH HEAT
Drop macaroni into a big pot of boiling water.

7
Boil macaroni 10 minutes. Drain it well.

8
Put in a casserole. Pour hot mince over + serve.

COMBINATION NOODLES 🍄🍄🍄

Serves 4

85 g sachet prawn-
   flavoured noodles
1 cup water
2 tablespoons oil
100 g button mushrooms,
   thinly sliced
4 rashers bacon, chopped
½ medium red capsicum
1 small carrot, coarsely
   grated
130 g can corn kernels,
   drained
3 spring onions, chopped
½ cup bean sprouts
2 teaspoons dark soy
   sauce
1 tablespoon tomato sauce

1.
Cook noodles, flavour sachet and water in a small pan.

2.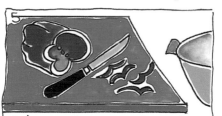
Stir until liquid is absorbed. Cover and put to one side.

3.
Heat oil in a big pan or wok.

4.
Add chopped mushrooms and bacon, stir 5 minutes.

5.
Cut capsicum in thin strips (throw away seeds). Add to pan.

6.
Add carrot, corn, spring onions and bean sprouts. Stir well.

7.
Add the cooked noodles, soy and tomato sauce. Stir well.

8.
Cook for 2 minutes until hot, stirring gently. Serve immediately.

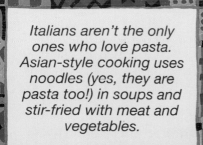
Italians aren't the only ones who love pasta. Asian-style cooking uses noodles (yes, they are pasta too!) in soups and stir-fried with meat and vegetables.

BIG PIZZA 👨‍🍳👨‍🍳👨‍🍳

Serves 4

2 cups self-raising flour
¼ teaspoon salt
30 g butter
1 cup milk
1 tablespoon oil
¼ cup tomato sauce

2 cups grated Cheddar
 cheese
1 tomato, thinly sliced
1 cup well drained
 pineapple pieces
1 cup finely chopped ham
 (or salami)

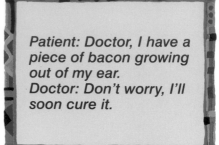

Patient: Doctor, I have a piece of bacon growing out of my ear.
Doctor: Don't worry, I'll soon cure it.

1 Turn oven to 220°C (425°F) Get out a large oven tray.

2 Sift flour + salt into bowl. Chop up butter and add.

3 Use your fingertips to rub together the flour and butter until they look like breadcrumbs.

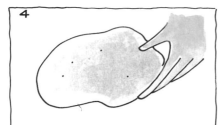

4 Add milk (more if needed) and knead + mix to a soft dough.

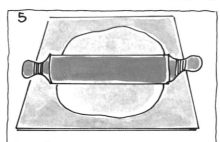

5 Roll it out on the baking tray until 34 cm in diameter

6 Brush dough with oil then the tomato sauce.

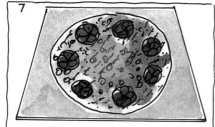

7 Sprinkle cheese over, arrange tomato slices on top.

8 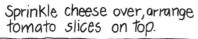 Spread pineapple and ham evenly over.

Bake 20-25 minutes or until cooked.

MEXICAN PITTA 👨‍🍳👨‍🍳

Makes 3
3 pitta breads
½ cup refried beans
½ cup taco sauce
½ cup grated mozzarella
cheese
½ medium green capsicum
9 black olives
9 corn chips
¼ cup sour cream

1. Turn oven to 200°C (400°F).

2. Grease a baking tray. Put pitta breads on tray.

3. Spread bread with beans. Top with taco sauce.

4. Chop capsicum finely (throw away seeds).

5. Sprinkle capsicum and grated cheese over sauce.

6. Arrange olives and chips on top.

7. Bake for 15 minutes.

8. Put a spoonful of sour cream in centre just before serving.

MEATY PIZZA WEDGES 🎩🎩

Serves 4

375 g minced beef
¼ cup dried breadcrumbs
1 teaspoon dried oregano
   leaves
1 small onion, grated
½ medium red capsicum
60 g salami
3 tablespoons tomato
   purée
1 large tomato, sliced
½ cup grated mozzarella
   cheese

1 Turn oven to 200°C (400°F).	**2** Put mince, breadcrumbs, oregano and onion in a big bowl.	**3** Chop capsicum and salami finely. Add to bowl.
4 Add tomato purée and a little salt and pepper.	**5** Use hands to knead mixture together.	**6** Grease a deep 23cm pie dish. Press mixture into dish.
7 Arrange tomato over pizza. Sprinkle with cheese.	**8** Bake 20 minutes. Pour off any liquid, slice and serve.	*You'll probably find you need a knife and fork to eat this meal – it's not really finger food.*

PINEAPPLE PAN PIZZA 👨‍🍳👨‍🍳

Serves 2

2 teaspoons oil
1 Lebanese bread
2 tablespoons tomato
  paste
½ teaspoon dried oregano
  leaves

100 g Cheddar cheese
80 g sliced ham
60 g pepperoni
2 canned pineapple rings,
  drained

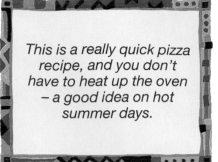

This is a really quick pizza recipe, and you don't have to heat up the oven – a good idea on hot summer days.

1

Grease a big non-stick pan with the oil.

2
Spread bread with tomato paste. Sprinkle on oregano.

3

Grate cheese coarsely. Sprinkle over bread.

4

Put bread in pan.

5

Cut ham and pepperoni into thin strips.

6

Arrange over bread.

7
Chop pineapple rings and arrange over pizza.

8

LOW HEAT
Cover pizza and cook gently for 8 minutes.

PIZZA SUPREME 👨‍🍳👨‍🍳

Serves 4

1 large pizza base
½ cup bottled spaghetti
    sauce
2 cups grated mozzarella
    cheese
1 onion
125 g button mushrooms
½ medium green capsicum
200 g can peeled prawns,
    drained
100 g cabanossi
100 g pepperoni
12 black olives, pitted

1 Turn oven to 200°C (400°F).

2 Grease pizza tray. Put pizza base on tray.

3 Spread with spaghetti sauce and ½ the cheese.

4 Cut onion, mushrooms and capsicum (throw away seeds) into thin slices.

5 Arrange vegetables on pizza.

6 Sprinkle prawns and remaining cheese over.

7 Slice cabanossi and pepperoni. Arrange on pizza with olives.

Cabanossi are long, skinny sausages with a mild garlicky flavour. Pepperoni has a peppery, hot flavour. If you don't like these, try ham or salami instead.

Bake 25 minutes. Serve hot.

MINCE 'N' MUSHROOM PIZZA 👨‍🍳👨‍🍳👨‍🍳

Serves 4

2 tablespoons oil
340 g packet scone mix
⅓ cup grated Cheddar
  cheese
125 g minced beef
200 g button mushrooms,
  thinly sliced
1 cup tomato purée
1 teaspoon dried mixed
  herbs
1 clove garlic, crushed
6 cherry tomatoes,
  cut in half
6 slices processed cheese,
  cut into thin strips
6 black olives

1 Turn oven to 200°c (400°F).	**2** Brush a 30cm × 20cm shallow pan with 1 tablespoon oil.

3 Follow directions on packet to make scone dough.

 **4** Knead cheese into dough. Press dough into tin.

5 Heat remaining oil in pan and cook mince until all red is gone.

 **6** Add mushrooms, tomato purée, mixed herbs and garlic. Simmer 10 minutes.

 Pour over scone base. Decorate with tomatoes, cheese and olives.

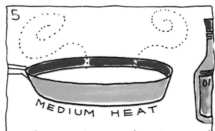 To peel garlic, cut garlic clove longways, then you can easily pull off the skin. To crush, cover with the wide, flat blade of a knife; hit the knife with your hand.

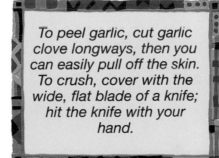 **8** Bake 25 minutes. Serve hot.

CHICKEN, MEAT AND SEAFOOD

These are substantial, main meal dishes that will really impress when you serve them up. You might like to accompany some recipes with your favourite vegetables. Add a luscious dessert from chapter six and you're sure to have a great success on your hands.

CHICKEN FILLET BURGERS 🧑‍🍳🧑‍🍳

Makes 2

1 egg, lightly beaten
¼ cup cornflour
1 cup cornflake crumbs
2 tablespoons desiccated
   coconut
2 chicken breast fillets
2 tablespoons oil
2 hamburger buns

1 banana, sliced diagonally
½ cup shredded lettuce
½ cup grated carrot
¼ cup alfalfa sprouts
¼ cup fruit chutney
⅓ cup grated Cheddar
   cheese

Burgers can be a really healthy, energy-giving meal – use lean minced meat, chicken or fish, be generous with the salad ingredients and use wholemeal buns.

1
Put egg and cornflour in a small bowl. Mix until smooth.

2
Put cornflake crumbs and coconut on a flat plate.

3
Dip chicken into egg mixture and then roll in crumbs.

4
MEDIUM HEAT
Heat oil in a big, heavy pan.

5
MEDIUM HEAT
Add chicken and cook 3 minutes. Turn and cook other side 3 minutes until golden.

6
Take out and put on paper towels to drain.

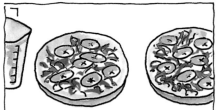

7
Open up buns. Put banana, lettuce, carrot and alfalfa on bottom halves.

8
Add chicken, chutney and grated cheese. Put top on. Serve immediately.

CRISPY CHICKEN ROLLS 👨‍🍳👨‍🍳

Makes 4

⅓ cup mango chutney

1 tablespoon sour cream

2 spring onions, finely chopped

8 sheets filo pastry

4 chicken breast fillets, skinless

60 g butter, melted

1
Turn oven to 180°c (350°F). Lightly grease an oven tray.

2
Put chutney, cream and spring onions in a small bowl. Mix well.

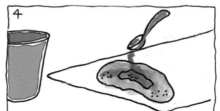
3
Lay out one sheet of filo pastry. Put another sheet on top. Fold in ½ longways.

4
Put a chicken fillet at one end. Spoon ¼ mango mixture onto chicken.

5
Roll pastry once over chicken. Fold sides over, and keep rolling to make a parcel.

6
Repeat to make 3 more chicken parcels.

7
Arrange parcels on tray and brush with melted butter.

8
Bake 20 minutes or until golden. Serve hot.

CHICKEN SATAYS 👨‍🍳👨‍🍳

Makes 12

6 chicken thighs, skinned, boned
2 teaspoons soy sauce
⅓ cup crunchy peanut butter
2 tablespoons lemon juice
150 g can coconut cream
1 tablespoon sweet chilli sauce
¼ teaspoon garam masala

1
Cut chicken in long, thin strips.

2
Put chicken and soy sauce in a bowl. Stir to cover chicken with sauce.

3
In another bowl, mix peanut butter and lemon juice together.

4
Add coconut cream, chilli sauce and garam masala. Mix well.

5
Mix 2 tablespoons peanut sauce into chicken.

6
Thread chicken onto skewers.

7
Grill for 3 minutes. Turn chicken and grill other side for 3 minutes.

Buy packets of bamboo or metal skewers from the supermarket. Soak the bamboo skewers in water to prevent them burning under the hot grill. Use gloves to pick up hot skewers.

8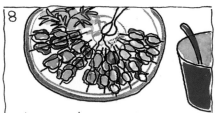
Put peanut sauce in a small pan. Cook 5 minutes until hot. Spoon over chicken and serve.

CHINESE LEMON CHICKEN ♟♟♟

Serves 4

12 chicken wings
1 stick celery
1 small carrot
1 medium red capsicum
3 teaspoons cornflour
2 teaspoons brown sugar
¼ teaspoon ground ginger
⅓ cup lemon juice
1 cup rich chicken stock

1 Wash chicken wings and pat dry.

2 Tuck wingtips under.

3 Put cornflour, sugar, ginger and lemon juice in a pan. Mix until smooth.

4 Cut celery, carrot and capsicum (throw away seeds) into long thin strips.

5 Add to cornflour mixture. Pour in chicken stock.

6 Stir until sauce boils and thickens.

7 Grill chicken for 8 minutes; turn and cook other side 8 minutes until golden.

8 Put chicken on a serving plate. Pour sauce over. Serve hot with rice.

CHICKEN WINGS 🐔🐔

Serves 4

2 tablespoons lemon juice
⅓ cup soy sauce
¼ teaspoon finely grated
  fresh ginger
10 chicken wings
2 tablespoons honey
2 tablespoons tomato
  sauce

1

Mix lemon juice, soy sauce + ginger in a large flat dish.

2
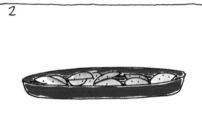
Add chicken wings, turning each till coated in sauce.

3

Cover dish and leave in fridge about 5 hours.

4

Drain the wings – save the sauce.

5

In a cup mix honey, tomato sauce + rest of soy sauce mix.

6

Grill the wings for 5 minutes. Brush them thickly with the honey mixture.

7

Grill 5 minutes more. Turn wings over, brush with more honey mixture.

8

Grill for 10 minutes more. Serve hot or cold.

CHICKEN AND GINGER ♙♙♙

Serves 6

2 whole chicken breasts
1 teaspoon cornflour
sprinkle of salt and pepper
1 onion, finely chopped
1 stick celery, sliced
2 teaspoons finely grated
    fresh ginger
¼ teaspoon sugar
1 tablespoon sherry
2 tablespoons water
2 tablespoons oil
1 cup thinly sliced green
    beans

1. Cut chicken meat from bones. Slice the meat thinly.

2. Put in bowl. Stir in cornflour salt + pepper. Set it aside.

3. Put chopped onion + celery in another bowl.

4. Add ginger, sugar, sherry + water to onion + celery. Mix.

5. Heat oil in big frypan or a wok.
HIGH HEAT

6. Fry chicken, stirring it until cooked.
MEDIUM HEAT

7. Add onion + celery mixture. Fry it all, stirring, till cooked.
MEDIUM HEAT

8. Add beans. Cook stirring till they are hot. Serve.
MEDIUM HEAT

A glutton who came from
the Rhine
Was asked at what hour
he would dine.
He replied, 'At eleven,
At three, five, and seven,
And eight and a quarter
to nine.'

CHICKEN AND VEGETABLES 👨‍🍳👨‍🍳

Serves 4

3 chicken breast fillets
1 tablespoon oil
2 cups frozen stir-fry
  vegetables
1 tablespoon cornflour

1 tablespoon sherry
¼ cup pineapple juice
¼ cup water
½ cup drained pineapple
  pieces

The earliest cookbook still in existence was written by a Roman called Apicius some 2000 years ago. Apicius got his name from greedily shouting, 'I've none left, give me a piece o' yours!'

1
Chop the chicken into bite-size pieces.

2
Heat the oil in a big frypan.

3
Fry chicken, stirring, until golden + just cooked.

4
Add vegetables. Cook for 5 minutes, stirring.

5
Mix cornflour, sherry, juice and water in a cup.

6
Add, stirring until it's thickened and boiling.

7
Add pineapple. Stir it in.

8
Bring to the boil, stirring. Serve on rice.

GRILLED CHICKEN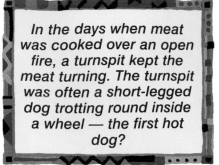

Serves 4

1 cup orange juice
2 teaspoons grated orange
  rind
½ teaspoon dry mustard
½ teaspoon ground nutmeg
¼ teaspoon curry powder

1 tablespoon chopped
  parsley
½ teaspoon instant chicken
  stock powder
sprinkle of salt and pepper
4 chicken breast fillets

In the days when meat was cooked over an open fire, a turnspit kept the meat turning. The turnspit was often a short-legged dog trotting round inside a wheel — the first hot dog?

1. Put orange juice, rind + mustard into a shallow dish.

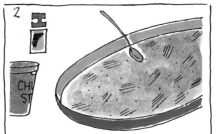

2. Mix in nutmeg, curry, parsley + chicken stock. Stir well.

3. Add salt + pepper. Add chicken coating it well with juice.

4. Cover the dish with some waxed paper.

5. Put it in fridge for 2 or 3 hours, turning chicken about 2 or 3 times.

6. Take out chicken. Put it under the grill.

7. Grill it slowly, turning chicken often so it won't burn. Grill about 30 minutes.

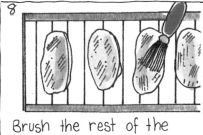

8. Brush the rest of the marinade over chicken as it's cooking.

SAVOURY PIE 👨‍🍳👨‍🍳👨‍🍳

Serves 4

1 small onion
1 x 500 g can minced beef
½ cup uncooked rice
1 cup tomato purée
sprinkle of salt and pepper
3 slices bread
30 g butter

1
Chop the onion finely.
Put in a big saucepan.

2
Add mince, rice, tomato
purée, salt and pepper.

3
Mix it all together very
well.

4
MEDIUM HEAT
Bring it to the boil,
stirring it all the time.

5
LOW HEAT
Simmer gently for 30 minutes
stirring now and then.

6
Spread evenly in big pie
dish or flat casserole.

7
Butter bread. Cut into tiny
cubes. Sprinkle on top.

8
Bake it at
180°C (350°F)
for 15 minutes,
then put it under grill
and grill for 5 minutes
or till top is crisp. ◀

HEARTY BEEF PIE ♟♟♟

Serves 4

500 g rump steak
2 tablespoons oil
500 g button mushrooms,
   cut in half
2 onions, sliced
2 tablespoons plain flour
1 teaspoon mixed dried
   herbs
1½ cups water
3 beef stock cubes,
   crumbled
2 teaspoons
   Worcestershire sauce
285 g packet flaky
   pastry mix

1. Turn oven to 180°C (350°F).

2. Cut steak into 2 cm cubes. Trim any fat off and throw away.

3. Heat oil in a deep, heavy pan. Add steak and cook, stirring for 5 minutes.

4. MEDIUM HEAT
Add mushrooms and onions. Stir 10 minutes until well browned.

5. MEDIUM HEAT
Stir in flour and herbs. Add water, stock cubes and sauce. Stir.

6. LOW HEAT
Put lid on and simmer for 30 minutes. Pour into a deep 23 cm pie dish.

7. Follow directions on packet to make pastry dough. Roll out to fit pie dish.

Don't peel or wash mushrooms before you use them, as this takes away flavour. Just wipe them with a damp cloth to remove any earth, then use as directed.

8. Cover dish with pastry. Make a few holes with a fork. Bake for 20 minutes.

SAUSAGE PIE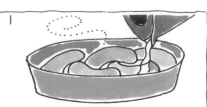

Serves 6

6 sausages
boiling water
375 g puff pastry
4 eggs
sprinkle of salt and pepper

1

Put sausages in a pan. Pour boiling water over. Leave until cool.

2

When cool, carefully peel the skin from the sausages.

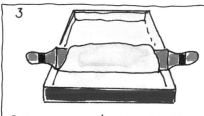

3

Cut pastry in half. Roll half out and line a 25 cm square tin with it.

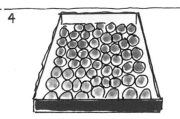

4

Slice up sausages. Arrange evenly in the tin.

5

Beat eggs, salt + pepper. Gently pour over sausages

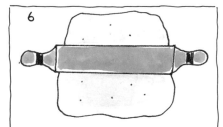

6

Roll out rest of pastry to make a lid. Place over sausages.

7

Seal the edges well. Prick top with a fork.

8

Bake it at 190°C (375°F) for 45 minutes.

Serve hot or cold

SAUSAGE AND BEAN BAKE

Serves 4

1 large onion
3 slices bacon,
2 sticks celery, sliced
4 continental sausages,
   sliced
2 spring onions, finely
   chopped

1 tablespoon finely
   chopped parsley
225 g can baked beans in
   tomato sauce
1 tablespoon tomato paste
½ cup water

Serve this dish with a crispy green salad and hot bread rolls. Put rolls on an oven tray; place in the oven for the last 15 minutes of cooking time.

1 Turn oven to 180°c (350°F).

2 Chop onion and bacon finely. (Throw away bacon rind.)

3 Mix onion, bacon, celery and sausage in a big bowl.

4 Add spring onions and parsley. Mix well.

5 Stir in baked beans, tomato paste and water.

6 Spread mixture into a shallow ovenproof dish.

7 Put lid on or cover with foil. Bake 20 minutes.

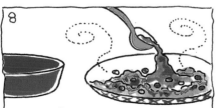

8 Take off lid or foil and bake for 15 minutes more. Serve hot.

SWEET AND SOUR MEATBALLS 👨‍🍳👨‍🍳👨‍🍳

Serves 4

MEATBALLS
500 g lean minced beef
2 tablespoons plain flour
¼ teaspoon salt
2 tablespoons oil

SAUCE
1 small onion
1 green capsicum
1 tablespoon oil
1 tablespoon cornflour
1 tablespoon soy sauce
1 tablespoon brown vinegar
2 tablespoon brown sugar
1 cup pineapple pieces
½ cup pineapple juice

1  Shape mince into about 16 meatballs. Roll them in the mixed flour and salt.	**2** Heat the 2 tablespoons oil. Gently fry, turning often, for about 20 minutes.	**3** Meanwhile, peel + chop the onion. Slice green capsicum Throw away the seeds.
4 Heat the 1 tablespoon oil in saucepan. Fry onion and capsicum for 3 mins.	**5** Mix cornflour, soy sauce, vinegar, brown sugar, pineapple + juice in a bowl.	**6** Add it all to saucepan + bring to boil, stirring it constantly. Simmer 2 mins.
7 Drain the cooked meatballs. Arrange them on a big platter of hot, cooked, rice.	*Try eating Chinese-style food with the traditional chopsticks — it can be an entertaining experience and it is sure to keep the Chinese laundry in business!*	**8** Pour the sauce all over the meatballs. Serves 4 people.

CRISPY TEX-MEX CASSEROLE 👒👒👒

Serves 6

1 tablespoon oil
500 g minced beef
410 g can tomatoes,
   crushed
425 g can red kidney beans
¼ teaspoon cumin
500 g potatoes, thinly sliced
1 cup grated Cheddar
   cheese
50 g packet corn chips

1 Heat oil in a big, heavy pan. Fry mince 5 minutes.

2 Add tomatoes, drained kidney beans + cumin. Stir.

3 LOW HEAT Turn down heat and simmer 15 minutes, stirring every now and then.

4 Turn oven to 180°c (350°F). In a bowl mix potatoes with ½ the cheese.

5 Layer ⅓ of the potatoes on base of an ovenproof dish. Spoon ½ the mince on top.

6 Top with another potato layer, another mince layer and finish with potatoes.

7 Bake for 45 minutes.

8 Spread rest of cheese + the chips over top. Bake for 15 minutes more.

"Tex-Mex" means a dish with the typical flavours of Texas and Mexico, usually beans, beef, corn, cheese, cumin (a herb) and sometimes chilli.

BEEF CASSEROLE

Serves 4

750 g lean stewing beef
½ cup plain flour
1 onion
1 carrot
1 beef stock cube
2 cups hot water
1 tablespoon tomato sauce

1 tablespoon
   Worcestershire sauce
1 tablespoon brown sugar
1 tablespoon vinegar
½ teaspoon ground
   nutmeg
sprinkle of salt and pepper

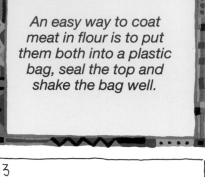

An easy way to coat meat in flour is to put them both into a plastic bag, seal the top and shake the bag well.

1 Turn oven to 180°C (350°F). Trim fat from the beef.

2 Slice the beef into bite-size cubes.

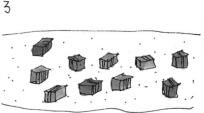

3 Toss beef in flour until each piece is coated.

4 Put in casserole. Peel + chop onion + carrot and add.

5 Dissolve stock cube in hot water. Stir in the sauces.

6 Stir in brown sugar, vinegar, nutmeg, salt and pepper.

7 Pour it all into casserole. Put the lid on.

8 Bake for 2 hours.

74

HAMBURGER WITH THE LOT 👨‍🍳👨‍🍳👨‍🍳

Makes 4

500 g hamburger mince
110 g packet hamburger
    seasoning mix
¼ cup oil
1 large onion,
    sliced into rings
4 rashers bacon
4 eggs

4 hamburger buns
4 slices Cheddar cheese
1 cup shredded lettuce
1 medium tomato, sliced
8 slices beetroot, well
    drained
4 pineapple rings
⅓ cup tomato sauce

Wash lettuce well to get rid of dirt and any bugs that may be hiding among the leaves. Wash under running water and then dry with paper towels.

1. Mix mince and seasoning in a bowl. Shape into 4 patties.

2. Heat oil in a big, heavy pan. Fry patties 3 minutes, turn and cook other side 3 minutes

3. Drain on paper towels, cover and keep warm.

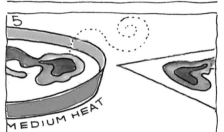

4. Fry onions until golden; drain on paper towels.

5. Fry bacon until crisp; drain on paper towels.

6. Fry eggs one at a time; keep warm.

7. Cut open buns. Toast until golden.

8. Lay everything on bun bottoms. Top with sauce, put top on and serve.

75

ASIAN BEEF AND VEGETABLES 👨‍🍳👨‍🍳👨‍🍳

Serves 6

750 g rump steak
2 spring onions, chopped
2 cloves garlic, crushed
2 tablespoons barbecue
  sauce
¼ cup oyster sauce
¼ teaspoon ground ginger
2 tablespoons oil
1 large onion, sliced
3 cups finely sliced
  vegetables (celery,
  broccoli, baby corn,
  carrot)

1. Trim any fat and throw it away. Cut beef into long, thin strips.

2. Put beef in a bowl. Add spring onions, garlic, barbecue and oyster sauces and ginger. Mix.

3. Heat oil in wok. Divide meat into 3 lots.

4. Add one lot of meat, stir quickly for 30 seconds.

5. Lift meat onto a plate. Repeat until all meat is cooked.

6. Add onion to wok. Stir for 2 minutes.

7. Add chopped vegetables. Stir for 3 minutes.

Stir-frying food seals in the goodness. To stir-fry, quickly move vegies or meat around the wok with a large spoon or spatula. Don't let them sit in the bottom as they will burn.

8. Add meat to wok. Stir for 5 minutes. Serve immediately with rice.

MEAT LOAF

Serves 6

1 kg lean minced beef
1 cup seasoned stuffing
   mix (from a packet)
1 cup tomato purée
1 egg
sprinkle of salt and pepper
2 tablespoons tomato
   sauce

1 Turn oven to 180°C (350°F) Put mince in a big bowl.

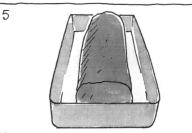
2 Add stuffing mix, puree, egg, salt and pepper.

3 Mix it, stirring very well until it is mixed and smooth.

4 With clean hands, shape it firmly into a loaf.

5 Put into a greased baking dish. Bake it for 1 hour.

6 Take out of oven. CAREFULLY tip away any fat.

7 Spread tomato sauce on top of loaf. Put back in oven.

8 Bake 30 minutes more. Serve hot or cold.

LAMB AND APRICOT PARCELS 👨‍🍳👨‍🍳

Makes 6
100 g dried apricots, finely
    chopped
500 g minced lamb
½ cup apricot conserve
½ cup herb stuffing mix
3 sheets ready-rolled puff
    pastry
1 egg, lightly beaten

1 Turn oven to 180°c (350°F).

2 Mix apricots, lamb, conserve and stuffing mix. Leave 20 minutes.

3 Shape mince into 6 flat, square patties, about 10cm × 10cm.

4 Cut pastry sheets in ½ to make 6 pieces. Put a pattie on the end of each piece.

5 Brush pastry with beaten egg.

6 Fold over pattie. Press edges together. Trim edges.

7 Cut 3 slits in top of each parcel with a sharp knife.

8 Brush with egg. Bake for 30 minutes until crisp and golden.

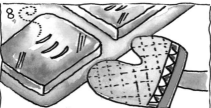

LAMB KEBABS

Serves 4
8 lamb chump chops
200 g carton plain yoghurt
2 cloves garlic, crushed
½ teaspoon ground turmeric
2 tablespoons tomato paste
2 tablespoons peanut butter
¼ teaspoon ground ginger
¼ teaspoon garam masala

1. Trim bones and any fat from chops and throw away.

2. Cut meat into 2 cm cubes.

3. Mix together yoghurt, garlic, turmeric, tomato paste, peanut butter, ginger + garam masala.

4. Add meat. Stir to cover meat with sauce.

5. Cover bowl with plastic wrap. Put in fridge for 2 hours.

6. Thread meat onto skewers.

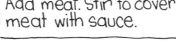

7. Grill kebabs 12 minutes. Turn frequently so all sides are cooked and browned.

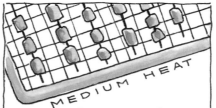

8. Serve hot with a salad.

LAMB HOT POT 🍳🍳

Serves 4

1 large onion
2 large carrots
250 g button mushrooms
2 large potatoes
8 lamb chump chops
410 g can tomatoes,
  crushed

¼ cup lemon juice
½ teaspoon dried oregano
  leaves
1 tablespoon chicken stock
  powder
½ cup tomato paste

This dish takes a while to cook, so add up the cooking times mentioned (45 + 20 mins = 1 hr 5 mins) and begin cooking 1 hour 5 minutes before you want to eat.

1

Turn oven to 180°c (350°F).

2

Chop onion and carrots. Cut mushrooms in half.

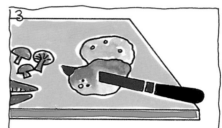

3

Cut each potato into cubes.

4

Trim fat from chops and throw away.

5

Put chopped vegetables, canned tomatoes and chops into a casserole dish.

6

Mix lemon juice, oregano, stock powder + tomato paste in a jug. Pour over meat + vegetables.

7

Put lid on or cover with foil. Bake 50-60 minutes.

8

Remove lid or foil, stir the casserole, and bake for 20 minutes more. Serve hot.

SPARERIBS IN PLUM SAUCE 🎩🎩

Serves 6

1 kg rack American-style
  pork spareribs
⅓ cup plum jam
1 tablespoon dark
  soy sauce
1 tablespoon Thai sweet
  chilli sauce
¼ teaspoon Chinese
  five-spice powder
3 teaspoons cornflour
½ cup chicken stock

1 Turn oven to 200°C (400°F).

2 Put ribs onto a rack in a shallow baking dish.

3 Bake for 25 minutes. Turn ribs once during cooking.

4 Heat jam, soy and chilli sauce and five-spice powder in a small pan.

5 Mix cornflour and chicken stock together until smooth.

6 Pour into pan. Stir gently until plum sauce boils and thickens.

7 When ribs are cooked, pull ribs apart. Arrange on a serving dish.

American-style spareribs are thinner and less fatty than pork spareribs. If you use pork spareribs for this recipe, trim most of the fat away before you cook them.

8 Pour plum sauce over. Serve immediately.

HAM AND PINEAPPLE 👨‍🍳👨‍🍳

Serves 4

4 canned pineapple rings
  in pineapple juice
2 tablespoons brown sugar
4 ham steaks (about 1 cm
  thick)
75 g butter

1
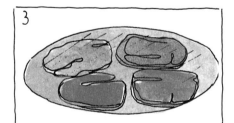
Drain pineapple rings.
Save ½ cup of the juice.

2
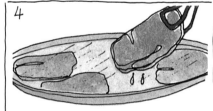
Put juice + brown sugar
in a large flat dish.

3

Put steaks in. Put in fridge.
Leave in fridge 3 hours.

4

Turn steaks over every
hour.

5

MEDIUM HEAT
Heat butter in large frying
pan. Drain the ham.

6

MEDIUM HEAT
Fry ham till golden.
Turn steaks often.

7

Fry pineapple for a few
minutes at the end.

8

Serve with a salad.
Serves 4 people.

SALMON PASTA POTS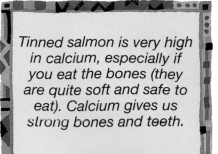

Serves 4

1 cup small spiral pasta
210 g can pink salmon
1 small carrot
1 spring onion, finely
  chopped
¼ cup mayonnaise

⅓ cup cream
½ red capsicum,
  finely chopped
2 tablespoons chopped
  parsley

Tinned salmon is very high in calcium, especially if you eat the bones (they are quite soft and safe to eat). Calcium gives us strong bones and teeth.

1 Boil a big pot of water. Carefully add spiral pasta.

2 Boil for 10 minutes. Drain well.

3 Turn oven to 180°c (350°F).

4 Tip salmon into a mixing bowl. Mash with a fork.

5 Grate carrot over salmon. Add spring onion.

6 Add pasta, mayonnaise, cream, capsicum and parsley to bowl.

7 Spoon mixture into 4 small ovenproof pots.

Bake for 15 minutes or until heated through. Serve hot.

FISH CAKES 👨‍🍳👨‍🍳👨‍🍳

Serves 6

500 g potatoes, peeled
15 g butter
1 x 210 g can pink salmon
1 egg
salt and pepper

1 onion, peeled and finely
  chopped
¼ cup fresh breadcrumbs
1 cup dry packaged
  breadcrumbs
2 tablespoons oil

1 Boil potatoes till tender. Drain well.

2 Add butter. Mash well till smooth.

3 Drain + flake fish. Add to potatoes. Add egg, salt, pepper, onion, fresh crumbs. Mix well.

4 With lightly floured hands, shape into cakes.

5 Put dry crumbs in a dish. Coat each fish cake in crumbs

6 Put them on a tray. Refrigerate for 1 hour.

7 Heat oil in a frypan.

8 Fry till golden on both sides Drain and serve.

FANCY FISH FINGERS

Serves 4

¹⁄₃ cup tomato relish
12 fish fingers
3 slices processed cheese
4 rashers bacon

1. Turn oven to 200°c (400°F).

2. Spread relish on one side of each fish finger.

3. Cut each cheese slice into 4 strips.

4. Lay a slice over relish.

5. Cut bacon into long thin strips.

6. Wrap bacon around each finger.

7. Place fingers on an oven tray (you don't need to grease the tray).

8. Bake 10 minutes. Serve hot.

FRIED RICE 🍄🍄🍄

Serves 4

1/3 cup oil
1 cup long-grain rice
1 1/2 cups chicken stock
1/2 cup frozen peas, rinsed and drained
1/2 medium red capsicum, finely sliced
100 g button mushrooms, thinly sliced
2 eggs, lightly beaten
2 spring onions, chopped
200 g can peeled prawns
1 tablespoon soy sauce
2 teaspoons sesame oil

1 Heat 2 tablespoons oil in a pan. Add rice. Stir 5 minutes or until golden.

2 Pour in stock. Turn down heat, put lid on. Simmer 15 minutes or until rice is tender.

3 Add peas. Cover and put to one side.

4 Heat 1 tablespoon oil in wok. Add capsicum. Stir 1 minute. Drain on paper towels.

5 Add rest of oil. Add mushrooms. Stir 1 minute. Drain with capsicum.

6 Add eggs. Swirl over base — don't stir.

7 When cooked like an omelette, lift out and slice.

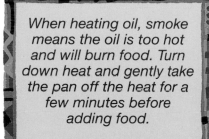

When heating oil, smoke means the oil is too hot and will burn food. Turn down heat and gently take the pan off the heat for a few minutes before adding food.

8 Put all ingredients into wok. Add soy sauce and sesame oil. Stir until hot.

SALMON MORNAY 👨‍🍳👨‍🍳👨‍🍳

Serves 4

1½ cups cooked rice
1 x 210 g can pink salmon
1 hard-boiled egg
50 g butter
2 tablespoons plain flour
1½ cups milk
⅓ cup grated cheddar
    cheese
sprinkle of salt and pepper
¼ cup dry breadcrumbs

1  Turn oven to 180°C (350°F) Spread rice in baking dish.	2  Drain salmon. Remove bones. Chop up. Spread on rice.	3  Chop egg. Sprinkle over the salmon. Melt butter in a small pan.
4  Stir in flour until smooth. Take off heat. Stir in milk.	5  Reheat, stirring all the time until it boils.	6 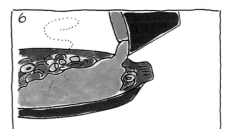 Stir in cheese, salt and pepper. Pour it over the salmon and rice.
7  Sprinkle crumbs evenly over. Bake for 20 minutes.	Tuna may be used instead of pink salmon for this recipe.	8 Serve it hot with a tossed salad Serves 4

TUNA LOAF 🍄🍄🍄

Serves 4

425 g can tuna
440 g can creamy
   mushroom soup
2 eggs
1½ cups cooked rice
1 small onion, finely chopped
1 celery stick, sliced
¼ cup chopped parsley
1 small grated carrot

1 Turn oven to 210°c (425°F). Grease a loaf tin well.

2 Line the tin with baking paper that hangs out over the 2 long sides – YOU'LL SEE WHY LATER

3 Drain the tuna well. Flake it with a fork.

4 Put tuna in mixing bowl. Stir in the soup.

5 Add the eggs, rice, onion, celery parsley and carrot. Mix well.

6 Spread it evenly into tin. Bake for 50 minutes.

7 Lift it out of the tin and onto a plate, using the baking paper.

A canner, exceedingly canny,
One morning remarked to his granny:
'A canner can can
Anything that he can,
But a canner can't can a can, can he?'

8 Turn out onto a plate, slice and serve with lemon wedges and a salad.

CHAPTER FOUR

MICROWAVE

The microwave oven makes cooking simple and convenient. The yummy recipes in this chapter cover soup, main meal dishes, puddings and cakes. Don't forget to read the special microwave cooking instructions at the front of the book before you start.

PEA AND HAM SOUP 👨‍🍳👨‍🍳

Serves 4-6

500 g smoked ham pieces
1 large onion, diced
500 g packet green split peas
1½ litres water

1
Put the ham, onion, peas and water in a deep microwave dish.

2
Cover and cook on Medium /High for 30 minutes, or until the peas are soft.

3
Stir the soup occasionally while it cooks.

4
Take out the ham. Chop up the meat and throw away the bones.

5
Mash soup lightly with a potato masher. If you want the soup thinner use a blender or add water.

6
Put the pieces of ham back into the soup.

7
When you are ready to eat, reheat the soup in the microwave 4-5 mins. on High.

8
Serve the soup with crusty bread.

CHICKEN AND CORN SOUP 👨‍🍳 👨‍🍳

Serves 6

3 teaspoons chicken stock powder
3½ cups boiling water
1 cup chopped cooked chicken
1 cup canned cream-style sweet corn

2 teaspoons cornflour
a little cold water
1 tablespoon chopped parsley
sprinkle of pepper

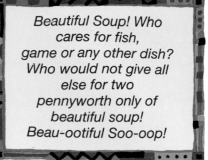

Beautiful Soup! Who cares for fish, game or any other dish? Who would not give all else for two pennyworth only of beautiful soup! Beau-ootiful Soo-oop!

1 Put stock powder + boiling water in a big bowl.

2 Add chicken + canned corn. Stir well.

3 Cover with a paper towel.

4 Microwave on High for 6-6½ minutes until boiling — stirring once.

5 Mix cornflour + cold water in a cup until smooth.

6 Stir in to soup. Stir well. Cover with paper towel.

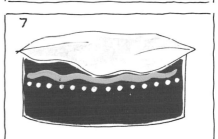

7 Bring to boil — microwave on High for 1½-2 minutes.

8 Stir in parsley and pepper. Serve.

HAM AND CHEESE BREAD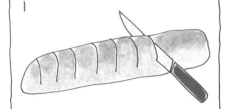

Serves 6

1 French stick (about 25 cm long)

8–10 slices cheese, thinly sliced

8–10 slices ham

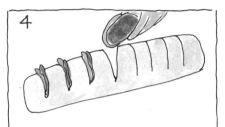

1. Slice French bread (not quite through) 8 or 10 times.

2.  Trim cheese to about the size of diameter of bread.

3.  Trim ham to about the same size.

4. Place ham + cheese together in each cut.

5. Put on a paper towel.

6. 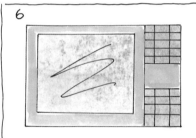 Cook on High 1–2 minutes.

7. Watch for cheese to start melting, then take out.

8.  Serve cut through.

GARLIC BREAD 🍞

Serves 6-8

1 loaf French bread (about
   60 cm long)
3 cloves garlic
100 g butter
ground pepper
1 tablespoon chopped
   parsley

1

Cut the French bread
in half.

2

Slice 2 cm apart - don't
cut through bottom crust.

3

Peel garlic cloves - crush
them with flat side of knife.

4

Put crushed garlic in a
small bowl. Add butter.

5
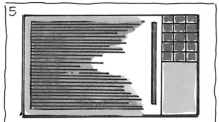
Soften butter - about 40
seconds on Low (30% power)

6

Add pepper, parsley.
Mash well with a fork.

7

Spread butter evenly onto
one side of each slice

8

Wrap each half loosely in
wax paper.
Cook each half separately
on High for 1 minute.

CHEESY SAUSAGE SLICE 👨‍🍳

Serves 4

4 slices wholemeal bread,
  buttered one side
2 continental frankfurts
  or 1 stick cabanossi
1 small onion
1 small zucchini
1 tablespoon self-raising
  flour
2 teaspoons finely chopped
  parsley
2 eggs, lightly beaten
½ cup grated mozzarella
  cheese

1
Cut crusts off bread.

2
Arrange, butter side up,
on bottom of a shallow,
round 23cm dish.

3
Cut frankfurts or
cabanossi into thin slices.

4
Coarsely grate onion and
zucchini into a bowl.

5
Add frankfurts or cabanossi,
flour and parsley.
Mix well.

6
Add eggs and cheese.
Stir well.

7
Spoon over bread. Cover
with plastic wrap.

8
Cook on a rack on Medium
High for 8 minutes. Serve
hot or cold.

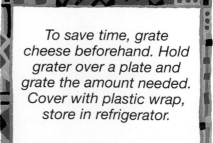

*To save time, grate
cheese beforehand. Hold
grater over a plate and
grate the amount needed.
Cover with plastic wrap,
store in refrigerator.*

CHEESE SNACK

Serves 1

1 slice of bread
2 teaspoons tomato sauce
   or chutney
cheese

1
Toast the bread.

2
Spread with tomato sauce.

3
Slice cheese thinly.

4
Cover sauce with cheese.

5
Put on a plate.

6
Cook on High for
18-20 seconds.

7
Watch it - take out when
cheese melts.

8
Serve.

CREAMY CHICKEN 👨‍🍳👨‍🍳

Serves 4

4 chicken breast fillets
½ teaspoon sweet paprika
1 onion, peeled and
  chopped
1 apple, peeled and
  chopped

1 x 440 g can cream of
  mushroom soup
½ teaspoon curry powder
¾ cup milk

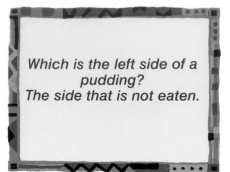

Which is the left side of a
pudding?
The side that is not eaten.

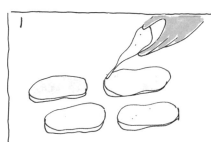

1. Take skin off chicken. Put in one layer in a dish.

2. Sprinkle with paprika.

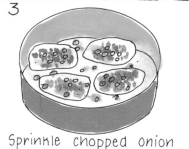

3. Sprinkle chopped onion + apple over.

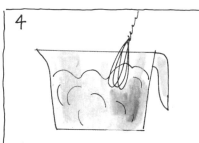

4. Mix soup, curry, milk well in a jug.

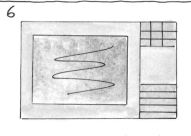

5. Pour over chicken. Cover with cling wrap. Prick.

6. Cook on Medium (70%) for 15 minutes.

7. Take out. Spoon the sauce over.

8. Cover again. Cook on Medium (70%) for 8-10 minutes.

MICROWAVE WINGS 🍗🍗

Serves 4

10 chicken wings
¾ cup plum sauce
1 tablespoon soy sauce
1 tablespoon tomato sauce
1 teaspoon brown sugar
2 teaspoons sesame seeds

1 Put wings in one layer in a dish.

2 Mix plum, soy and tomato sauces and sugar.

3 Pour it evenly over wings. Cover.

4 Stand 2 hours. Turn wings over once.

5 Cover with cling wrap. Pierce holes in it.

6 Cook on High for 6 minutes.

7 Turn wings over. Cook on Medium 5 minutes.

8 Stand 2 minutes. Sprinkle with seeds. Cool.

SAVOURY RICE RING 🍳

Serves 4-6

3 rashers bacon
1½ cups cooked long-grain
   rice
190 g can mushrooms,
   drained and thinly sliced
1 medium zucchini,
   coarsely grated
1 large carrot, coarsely
   grated
4 eggs, lightly beaten
1½ cups grated Cheddar
   cheese

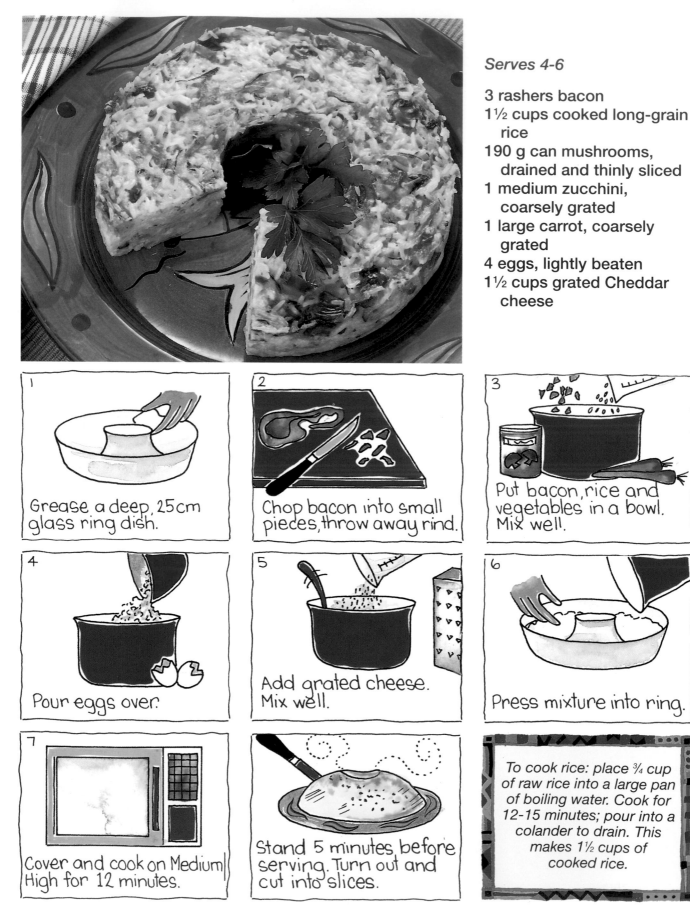

1. Grease a deep, 25cm glass ring dish.

2. Chop bacon into small pieces, throw away rind.

3. Put bacon, rice and vegetables in a bowl. Mix well.

4. Pour eggs over.

5. Add grated cheese. Mix well.

6. Press mixture into ring.

7. Cover and cook on Medium High for 12 minutes.

8. Stand 5 minutes before serving. Turn out and cut into slices.

To cook rice: place ¾ cup of raw rice into a large pan of boiling water. Cook for 12-15 minutes; pour into a colander to drain. This makes 1½ cups of cooked rice.

EASY APRICOT CHICKEN 👨‍🍳👨‍🍳

Serves 4

1 tablespoon flour
40 g sachet French onion
   soup mix
8 chicken drumsticks
   (about 1 kg)
2 medium zucchini,
   chopped
1 large onion, coarsely
   grated
½ teaspoon grated lemon
   rind
¾ cup apricot nectar
425 g can apricot halves,
   drained

1
Put flour and soup mix in a plastic bag.

2
Add chicken. Hold top firmly and shake until well coated.

3
Put chicken in a shallow dish.

4
Top with zucchini.

5
Stir onion, lemon rind and apricot nectar together.

6
Pour over chicken and zucchini.

7
Arrange apricots on top.

To grate lemon rind, use the side of the grater with the smallest holes. Hold over a plate and gently rub lemon skin. Don't press too hard or you'll get the bitter white pith.

8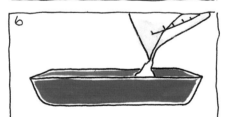
Cover and cook on Medium/High for 30 minutes. Stir once during cooking.

SPICY LAMB CURRY 👩‍🍳👩‍🍳

Serves 4

2 tablespoons oil
1 large onion, thinly sliced
2 teaspoons curry powder
¼ teaspoon garam masala
½ teaspoon dried coriander
    leaves
1 medium apple, chopped
750 g lamb chump chops,
    boned, cut into 3 cm
    pieces
1 large carrot, chopped
150 g can coconut cream
½ cup rich chicken stock
12 pappadums

1
Put oil and onion in a deep dish. Cook on High for 2 minutes.

2
Add curry powder, garam masala and coriander. Cook on High for 1 minute.

3
Add apple, lamb and carrot. Mix gently.

4
Stir in coconut cream and stock.

5
Cover and cook on Medium/High for 25 minutes. Stir halfway through cooking.

6
Leave 10 minutes before serving.

7
Put 2 pappadums in microwave. Cook on High until they puff up.

Pappadums are like large chips – light, crispy and delicious. They are made from lentil flour and they "grow" as they cook. Buy them from the supermarket.

8
Repeat until all pappadums are cooked. Serve with curry and rice.

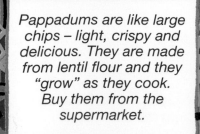

BEEF STROGANOFF 👨‍🍳👨‍🍳

Serves 4

1 tablespoon oil
1 large onion, thinly sliced
200 g baby mushrooms,
    thinly sliced
½ cup water
1 chicken stock cube,
    crumbled
2 teaspoons tomato paste
1 teaspoon French mustard
1 tablespoon sour cream
500 g rump steak cut into
    thin flat strips
1 tablespoon plain flour
2 teaspoons paprika

1. Put oil, onion and mushrooms in a deep casserole dish.

2. Cover and cook on High for 3 minutes. Stir.

3. Take off lid, cook on High for 3 minutes. Stir.

4. Put water, stock cube, tomato paste, mustard and cream in a jug. Mix well.

5. Pour over onion and mushrooms. Stir.

6. Cover and cook on High for 3 minutes.

7. Mix flour, paprika and a little pepper on a flat plate. Coat meat with mixture.

8. Add meat to dish. Stir. Cover and cook on Medium for 10 minutes. Serve with rice.

When serving, add an extra dollop of sour cream and some chopped chives to make this dish extra-special.

103

MINI MINCE CUPS

Makes 6

500 g pork and veal mince
500 g minced beef
40 g packet Savoury Mince
　　Seasoning Mix
130 g can diced capsicum,
　　drained
3 spring onions, finely
　　chopped

1 tablespoon chopped
　　fresh basil
1 egg, lightly beaten
2 tablespoons tomato paste
ready-made taco sauce,
　　to serve

1 Brush 6 small microwave dishes with oil.	**2**  Put the mince, Seasoning Mix, capsicum, spring onions and basil in a big bowl.	**3**  Add the egg and tomato paste.
4 Knead with your hands until it is all mixed in and smooth	**5**  Cover with plastic wrap and put in the fridge for 1 hour.	**6**  Press the mixture evenly into the dishes.

7 Cook on the microwave rack on Medium/High for 10 minutes.

8 Leave to stand for 5 minutes. Turn out onto plates and serve with sauce.

FRENCH VEGETABLES 👨‍🍳👨‍🍳

Serves 4

1 onion
1 teaspoon oil
½ green capsicum
3 zucchini
3 tomatoes
½ teaspoon dried basil
ground pepper

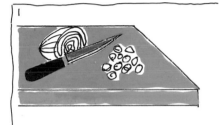

1

Peel onion. Chop finely. Put in large casserole.

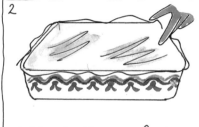

2

Add oil. Cover Cook on High for 2 minutes.

3

Chop up the green capsicum. Discard the seeds.

4

Stir in to casserole. Cover. Cook on High 2 minutes.

5

Slice zucchini thinly. Peel + chop tomatoes.

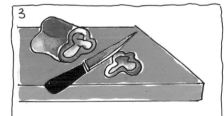

6

Add to the casserole. Stir in the basil

7

Cover with cling wrap. Cook on High 6 minutes.

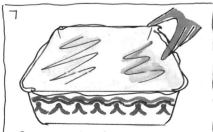

8

Gently stir in pepper. Serve.

SPANISH OMELETTE 👨‍🍳👨‍🍳👨‍🍳

Serves 4

1 small onion, finely
  chopped
15 g butter
1 cooked potato, chopped
1 tomato, chopped

1 small green capsicum,
  finely chopped
sprinkle of salt and pepper
3 eggs
2 tablespoons milk

1. Put chopped onion + butter in a bowl.

2. Cover with cling wrap. Prick. Microwave on High for 2 minutes.

3. Add potato, tomato, capsicum salt + pepper.

4. Add eggs + milk. Stir it all well.

5. Pour into a greased 20 cm pie plate.

6. Cover with cling wrap. Prick. Microwave on High for 1½ minutes.

7. Stir cooked egg to centre. Cover. Cook on High 1¾ minutes.

8. Stir again. Cook (uncovered) 1 minute. Stand 2 mins. Serve.

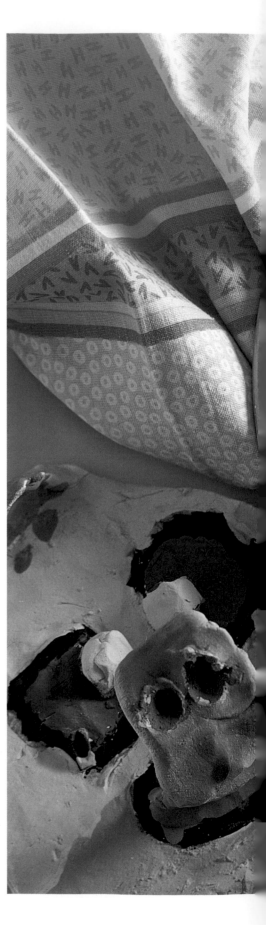

CHEESE AND POTATO BAKE 👨‍🍳👨‍🍳

Serves 6

30 g butter
1 onion, peeled and
    chopped
6 medium-sized potatoes
sprinkle of salt and pepper
⅔ cup milk
¾ cup grated Cheddar
    cheese

1
Put butter + onion in a bowl.
Cook on High 3 minutes.

2
Peel the potatoes.   Slice them
up thinly.

3
Put half the potatoes into a 22cm
round   casserole.

4
Spread onion + butter over.
Sprinkle with salt + pepper.

5
Arrange rest of potatoes evenly
over.

6
Pour the milk over.
Sprinkle cheese on top.

7
Cover with cling wrap. Prick.
Microwave on High for
8 minutes.

8
Remove cover.
Microwave on High
for 10 minutes
or until tender.

If you like, put under
grill to brown cheese
and serve.

CABBAGE BAKE 👨‍🍳👨‍🍳

Serves 4

3 cups shredded cabbage
2 tablespoons water
1 cup tinned tomatoes + juice
¼ cup grated cheese
1 cup shredded ham
1 tablespoon chopped parsley

1 Put cabbage + water in a 20 cm casserole.

2 Cover with cling wrap. Cook on High 6 minutes.

3 Roughly chop up the tinned tomatoes

4 Pour over hot cabbage. Stir gently.

5 Sprinkle with the grated cheese.

6 Stir the ham and parsley through.

7 Cover with cling wrap.

8 Cook it on High for 2 minutes. Stir + serve.

APRICOT-STUDDED PUDDING 👨‍🍳👨‍🍳

Serves 4-6

½ cup finely chopped dried
   apricots
⅓ cup fresh orange juice
6 slices wholemeal bread,
   buttered one side
¼ cup sugar
1 tablespoon custard
   powder

3 eggs, lightly beaten
½ teaspoon finely grated
   orange rind
1½ cups milk
1 tablespoon brown sugar
cream or ice-cream

This lovely bread pudding is also delicious made with dates instead of apricots.

Put apricots and juice in a small bowl. Cover and cook on Medium 4 minutes.

2
Cut crusts off bread. Cut each slice into small squares.

3
Arrange on bottom of a shallow ovenproof dish.

4
Put sugar, custard powder, eggs and rind in a bowl. Stir.

5
Put milk into big jug. Cook on High for 2 minutes or until very hot.

6
Pour onto egg mixture. Whisk until smooth.

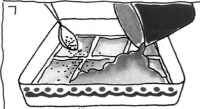
7
Pour gently over bread. Sprinkle with the apricots and brown sugar.

8
Cover. Cook on medium for 10 minutes. Leave to stand for 5 minutes.

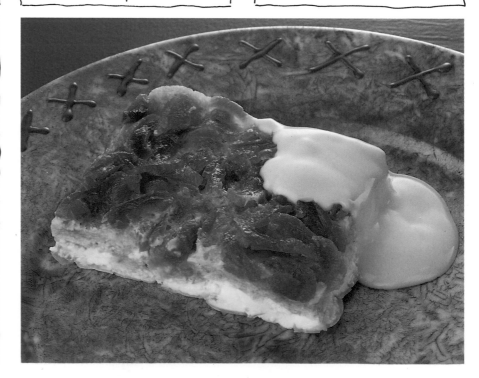

CHOCOLATE FUDGE SAUCE 🍮

Makes 2 cups

125 g dark chocolate, finely
    chopped
400 g can sweetened
    condensed milk
100 g white marshmallows

1 Put chocolate and condensed milk in a medium bowl.

2 Cook on Medium (50%) for 1 minute. Stir.

3 Cut marshmallows into small pieces.

4 Stir into chocolate mixture.

5 Cook on Medium (50%) for 1 minute.

6 Beat until almost smooth.

7 Cook on Medium (50%) for 1 minute. Stir.

8 Serve hot or cold with ice-cream.

BUTTERSCOTCH BANANAS 👨‍🍳

60 g butter   *Serves 4*
¼ cup brown sugar
¼ cup golden syrup
2 teaspoons lemon juice
2 tablespoons sour cream
3 bananas
2 tablespoons toasted
  flaked almonds
vanilla ice-cream

Put butter in a shallow, oblong dish. Cook on Medium for 45 seconds.

2

Add sugar and syrup. Stir until thick and smooth.

3

Cook on High for 2 minutes.

4

Add juice and cream. Stir well. Cook on High for 2 minutes.

5

Cut bananas in half longways and crossways.

6

Arrange in dish in 1 layer. Stir to coat with sauce.

7

Cook on Medium 4 minutes. Turn, cook 4 minutes more.

8

Sprinkle with almonds. Serve with ice-cream.

PAVLOVA ROLL

Serves 6

butter and cornflour to grease and dust tray
4 egg whites (at room temperature)
1 cup caster sugar
¾ teaspoon imitation vanilla essence

1 teaspoon white vinegar
½ cup toasted coconut, and more for Step 6
300 mL cream, whipped
1 cup sliced fruit, e.g. strawberries or banana

Did you know that there are only six things that you need to eat in order to be healthy? They are: carbohydrates, proteins, fats, water, minerals and vitamins. So why are you so spotty?

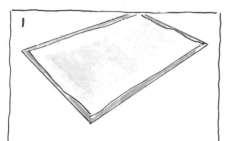
1. Grease lightly a 24×24cm micro dish. Line with paper.

2. Grease paper. Sprinkle with cornflour. Shake off excess.

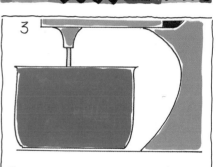
3. Beat egg whites until stiff.

4. Add sugar very slowly, beating all the time. Blend in vanilla + vinegar.

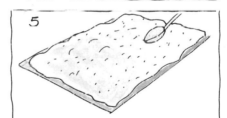
5. Spread evenly on tray. Sprinkle with coconut. Microwave on High for 2 minutes. Cool.

6. Sprinkle a sheet of waxed paper with more coconut. Turn cold pavlova onto it.

7. Spread with whipped cream and fruit.

8. Carefully roll up. Slide onto serving plate.

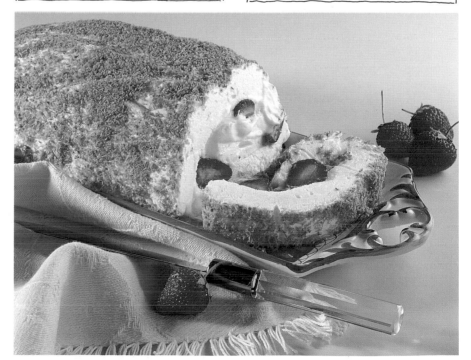

GOLDEN CARROT PUDDINGS

Makes 4

4 tablespoons golden syrup
60 g cold butter, cut into
    4 pieces
1⅓ cups coarsely grated
    carrot
½ cup chopped pecan nuts
½ cup sugar

⅔ cup wholemeal self-
    raising flour
½ teaspoon mixed spice
¼ teaspoon ground
    cinnamon
1 egg, lightly beaten
⅓ cup oil
whipped cream, to serve

*Whip cream in a blender, with electric beaters or with a whisk. Have the cream very cold
If you whip too long it will turn to butter: stop when it is just becoming thick and stiff.*

1 Lightly grease 4 microwave safe cups with oil.

2 Put a tablespoon of syrup into each cup. Put a piece of butter on top of it.

3  Put carrot, nuts and sugar in a bowl.

4  Sift flour, spice and cinnamon over.

5  Add egg and oil. Mix well.

6  Spoon evenly into cups. Smooth tops.

7  Cook on rack on Medium/High 6 minutes.

8  Leave in dish 5 minutes. Turn out. Serve with whipped cream.

HAZELNUT FUDGE CAKE

Serves 6

60 g butter
125 g dark chocolate,
  chopped
2 tablespoons hazelnut
  spread
2 eggs, lightly beaten
2 tablespoons sugar
½ cup self-raising flour
⅓ cup chopped hazelnuts
½ cup hazelnut spread,
  extra

1 Lightly grease a 20cm round cake dish.

2 Put butter and chocolate in a medium bowl.

3 Cook on Medium for 1 minute. Stir until smooth.

4 Add hazelnut spread, eggs, sugar, flour and nuts. Mix well.

5 Spread evenly in cake dish.

6 Cook on a rack on Medium/High for 4 minutes.

7 Leave in dish for 10 minutes, then turn out onto a serving plate.

8 Decorate top and sides with extra spread. Put in fridge for 20 minutes. Serve.

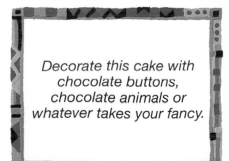
Decorate this cake with chocolate buttons, chocolate animals or whatever takes your fancy.

115

PINEAPPLE CAKE 👨‍🍳👨‍🍳

Makes 1 x 20 cm cake
60 g butter
¾ cup caster sugar
1 teaspoon imitation vanilla essence
1 egg
½ cup milk
1 cup crushed pineapple
½ cup coconut
1½ cups self-raising flour

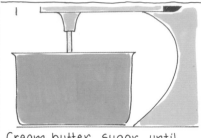
1 Cream butter, sugar until smooth.

2 Add vanilla and egg. Beat well.

3 Add milk, drained pineapple, coconut. Stir well.

4 Sift in self-raising flour. Mix well.

5 Pour into greased 20 cm ring mould - 7 cm deep.

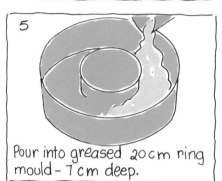
6 Microwave on rack for 7½-8 minutes on Medium (70%) uncovered.

7 Microwave on High for 4-4½ minutes more.

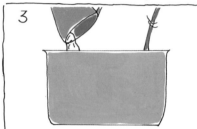

8 Stand 5 minutes. Tip out. Ice when cool. (See page 88)

MICROWAVE BUNS 👨‍🍳👨‍🍳

Serves 6

340 g packet scone mix
1 tablespoon brown sugar
½ teaspoon ground
    cinnamon
½ - ⅔ cup water
30 g butter, melted
1 cup mixed dried fruit
8 glacé cherries
1 tablespoon brown sugar,
    extra
PINK ICING
¾ cup icing sugar, sifted
2 teaspoons milk
60 g butter, melted
2 drops pink food colouring

1 Sift scone mix, sugar and cinnamon into a bowl.

2 Add enough water to mix to a soft dough.

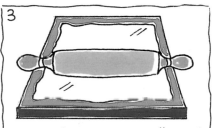

3 Turn out, knead gently, roll out to 30 × 35 cm.

4 Brush with butter, sprinkle with sugar and fruit.

5 Roll up, cut into 6 slices, arrange on round dish.

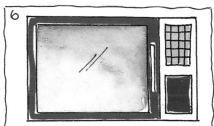

6 Cook on a rack on Medium/High 8 minutes.

7 Turn onto a wire rack to cool. Put cherries on top.

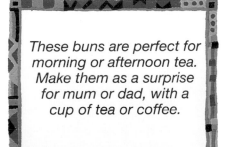

These buns are perfect for morning or afternoon tea. Make them as a surprise for mum or dad, with a cup of tea or coffee.

8 Mix sugar, milk, butter and colouring until smooth, drizzle over bun.

CHOCOLATE CRUNCH

Makes about 16 slices

180 g butter
1 cup cornflakes
1 cup desiccated coconut
¾ cup caster sugar
1 cup self-raising flour
2 tablespoons cocoa

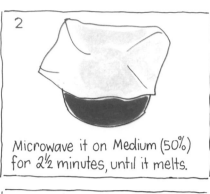
1
Put butter in small bowl.
Cover with paper towel.

2
Microwave it on Medium (50%)
for 2½ minutes, until it melts.

3
Put cornflakes, coconut,
sugar in a bowl.

4
Sift in flour + cocoa.

5
Add melted butter. Mix well.

6
Press firmly into greased
20 cm square dish.

7
Microwave on Medium High (90%)
for 5 minutes.

8
Ice with chocolate icing
while still warm.

SPIKY CRACKLES 🍫

Makes 16 squares

250 g packet jersey
    caramels, chopped
1 tablespoon golden syrup
60 g butter
250 g dark chocolate, finely
    chopped
3 cups Rice Bubbles
100 g white marshmallows,
    chopped
⅓ cup toasted slivered
    almonds

1

Line base and sides of a 23cm square dish with foil. (Don't put this in the microwave!)

2

Put caramels, golden syrup, butter and ½ the chocolate in a bowl.

3
Cook (uncovered) on Medium for 2 minutes. Stir until smooth.

4

Mix Rice Bubbles into caramel. Press into dish.

5

Put chocolate and marshmallows in a bowl.

6

Cook on Medium 45 seconds. Beat until smooth.

7

Spread over caramel mixture. Press nuts on top.

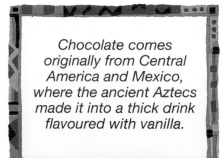
Chocolate comes originally from Central America and Mexico, where the ancient Aztecs made it into a thick drink flavoured with vanilla.

8

Leave to set, cut into fingers and serve.

CHAPTER FIVE
VEGETABLES AND SALADS

A host of fresh, crisp vegetables and salads, perfect partners to main meals. Try our zesty Mixed Salad, refreshing Tomato Salad or Corn Fritters.

BEAN SALAD

Serves 6

1 cup sliced cooked green
  beans, well drained
1 cup canned whole kernel
  corn, well drained
1 x 310 g can red kidney
  beans

¼ teaspoon sugar
¼ cup oil
¼ cup white vinegar
sprinkle of salt and pepper

*Diner: Waiter, what is this fly doing in my soup?
Waiter: The backstroke.*

1

Put the drained green beans
in a flat dish or bowl.

2

Add the drained corn.
Stir it through.

3

Open can of kidney beans.
Drain them well.

4

Add them to the dish.

5

Mix sugar, oil, vinegar well
till sugar is dissolved.

6

Add salt and pepper.
Stir well.

7

Pour it all over beans
+ corn in the dish.

8

Stir through. Chill
in fridge and serve.

POTATO SALAD 👨‍🍳👨‍🍳

Serves 6

6 medium potatoes
1 x 310 g can whole kernel
   corn
¼ cup chopped parsley
sprinkle of salt and pepper
1 tablespoon bottled
   French dressing
¼ cup mayonnaise

Scrub the potatoes until they are clean.

2

Boil them in water until tender.

3

When cool, peel them and cut into cubes.

4

Put cubes into a nice salad bowl.

5

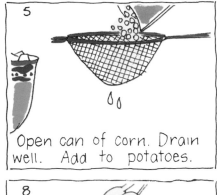

Open can of corn. Drain well. Add to potatoes.

6

Add the parsley, the salt and the pepper.

7

Stir in French dressing and the mayonnaise.

8

Gently mix it all and serve cold.

COLESAW 🍄🍄🍄

Serves 6

DRESSING
¾ cup evaporated milk
1 teaspoon sugar
¼ cup white vinegar
1 egg
sprinkle of salt and pepper

half a nice cabbage
2 medium carrots

1 Put milk, sugar, vinegar in a small saucepan.

2 Add egg, salt + pepper. Beat it till smooth.

3 Cook, stirring all the time, till it becomes thick.

4 Leave to cool. Pour into a jar and refrigerate.

5 Shred cabbage finely with a sharp knife.

6 Keep going carefully till you have 3 cupfuls.

7 Grate carrots. Toss with cabbage in salad bowl.

8 Toss with about ¾ cup of the dressing.
❀ Serves 6 people.

TOMATO SALAD

Serves 6

4 medium-sized ripe
  tomatoes

DRESSING
¼ cup oil
¼ cup white wine vinegar
¼ teaspoon French mustard
1 teaspoon caster sugar
cracked black pepper

Knock, knock.
Who's there?
Freeze.
Freeze who?
Freeze a jolly good fellow!

1. Wash and dry tomatoes. Slice them thinly.

2. Arrange them in a shallow dish.

3. Put the oil, vinegar, mustard and sugar in a jar with a screw-top.

4. Mix them all together by turning the jar upside-down. Make sure the lid is on tightly!

5. Pour the dressing evenly over the tomatoes.

6. Grind some black pepper over the salad using a pepper grinder, if you have one.

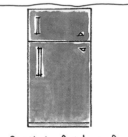

7. Cover. Chill in fridge for 1 hour, then serve.

8. You could try a different dressing: Mix ¼ cup peanut oil 2 tablespoons lemon juice 2 teaspoons soft brown sugar and 1 tablespoon chopped fresh basil.

MIXED SALAD 🍄🍄

Serves 6

8 button mushrooms
1 tablespoon chopped
   parsley
2 teaspoons lemon juice
2 tablespoons oil
3 zucchini

1 green capsicum
4 small tomatoes
5 leaves of mint
¼ cup bottled French
   dressing
freshly ground black
   pepper

1
Wipe mushrooms clean.
Slice them up thinly.

2
Put in bowl. Add parsley,
lemon juice and oil.

3
HIGH HEAT
Slice zucchini. Boil them
in water for 1 minute.

4
Drain well. Rinse in cold
water. Drain them again.

5
Chop the green capsicum
up very finely.

6
Chop the tomatoes up
into cubes. Chop up mint.

7
Put it all in a salad bowl.
Stir in the mushrooms.

8
Pour French dressing over.
Add pepper. Stir gently.
Chill till cold and serve.

GREEK SALAD 👨‍🍳👨‍🍳👨‍🍳

Preparation time:
20 minutes
Total cooking time: Nil
Serves 4

★

2 large or 3 small
vine-ripened tomatoes
1 green pepper
(capsicum)
1 Lebanese cucumber
250 g (8 oz) feta cheese
1 small red (Spanish)
onion, thinly sliced,
optional
⅓ cup (60 g/2 oz)
Kalamata olives
2–3 tablespoons lemon
juice
3–4 tablespoons olive oil

1 Carefully remove the small core from the top of each tomato. Cut each tomato into about 8 wedges.

2 Cut the pepper in half and remove the seeds and membrane. Cut the flesh into small squares.

3 Cut the cucumber in half lengthways and then into slices.

4 Cut the feta cheese into small cubes.

5 Combine the tomato, pepper, cucumber, onion (if using), cheese and olives in a large bowl. Drizzle with the lemon juice and oil. Sprinkle with salt and freshly ground black pepper. Stir gently to mix, then serve.

SCALLOPED POTATOES 👨‍🍳👨‍🍳👨‍🍳

Preparation time: 15 minutes
Total cooking time: 45 minutes
Serves 4

★

500 g (1 lb) potatoes
⅔ cup (170 ml/5½ fl oz) milk
½ cup (125 ml/4 fl oz) cream
½ cup (60 g/2 oz) grated Cheddar cheese
½ teaspoon ground nutmeg
20 g (⅔oz) butter

1 Brush a 20 cm (8 inch) square shallow ovenproof dish with melted butter or oil, and preheat the oven to moderate 180°C (350°F/Gas 4).

2 Peel the potatoes and cut them into thin slices.

3 Place the slices in layers in the prepared dish, overlapping the slices slightly.

4 Combine the milk and the cream in a jug, and drizzle the mixture over the potatoes.

5 Sprinkle the cheese evenly over the potato, then dust with the nutmeg and dot with butter.

6 Bake for 45 minutes, or until the potato is tender when tested with a knife and the top is golden brown.

GLAZED PUMPKIN

Serves 6

750 g pumpkin
salt and pepper
50 g butter
2 tablespoons golden syrup
½ cup fresh breadcrumbs

1
Turn oven to 180°C (350°F)
Grease a shallow baking dish.

2
Slice pieces of pumpkin about
3 cm thick. Trim off skin.

3
Arrange pieces in the
baking dish.

4
Sprinkle pieces with
salt and pepper.

5
Cover with a lid of foil.
Bake for 35 minutes.

6
LOW HEAT
Melt butter + golden syrup.
Stir in breadcrumbs.

7
Take foil lid off. Pour crumb
mixture all over pumpkin.

8
Bake it (uncovered) for
20 minutes more.

ONION AND TOMATO 👨‍🍳👨‍🍳

Serves 4

4 medium-sized onions
3 cups water
1 medium-sized tomato
sprinkle of salt and pepper
2 tablespoons cornflour
¼ cup cold water

1

Peel onions. Slice them into rings. Put in pan.

2
LOW HEAT
Add water. Bring to the boil. Simmer 20 minutes.

3
Drain off the liquid – save ¾ cup of it.

4

Slice tomato thinly. Add to onion with the liquid.

5

LOW HEAT
Add salt and pepper. Simmer 5 minutes.

6
Mix cornflour + cold water in a cup until smooth.

7

LOW HEAT
Gently stir it in until it comes to the boil.

8

Delicious served on fish or with steak.

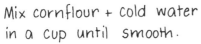

OVEN FRIES 👨‍🍳👨‍🍳👨‍🍳

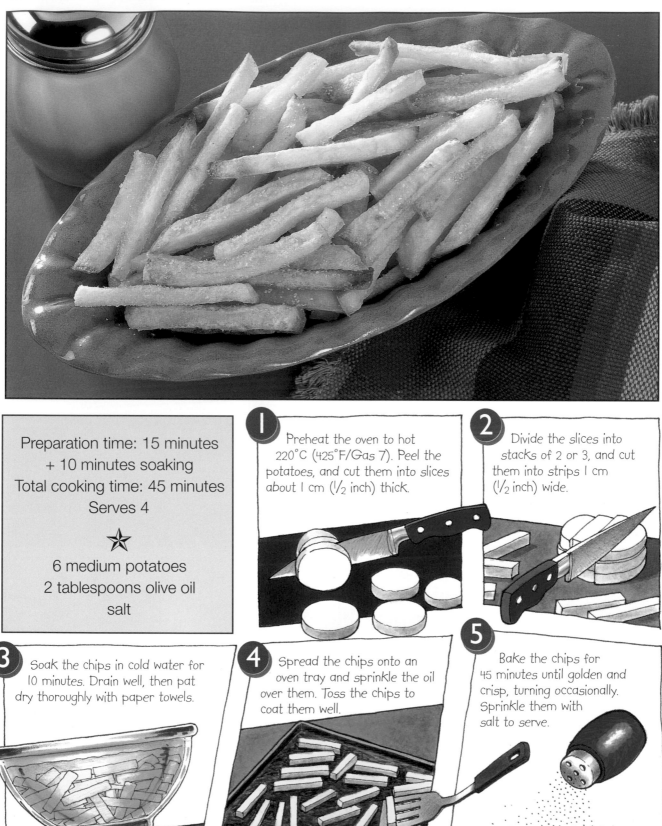

Preparation time: 15 minutes
+ 10 minutes soaking
Total cooking time: 45 minutes
Serves 4

★

6 medium potatoes
2 tablespoons olive oil
salt

1 Preheat the oven to hot 220°C (425°F/Gas 7). Peel the potatoes, and cut them into slices about 1 cm (½ inch) thick.

2 Divide the slices into stacks of 2 or 3, and cut them into strips 1 cm (½ inch) wide.

3 Soak the chips in cold water for 10 minutes. Drain well, then pat dry thoroughly with paper towels.

4 Spread the chips onto an oven tray and sprinkle the oil over them. Toss the chips to coat them well.

5 Bake the chips for 45 minutes until golden and crisp, turning occasionally. Sprinkle them with salt to serve.

VEGETARIAN CHILLI 👨‍🍳👨‍🍳👨‍🍳

1 Put the burghul in a heatproof bowl and pour in 1 cup (250 ml/8 fl oz) of hot water. Leave to stand until needed.

2 Heat the oil in a large pan and add the onion. Cook for about 10 minutes over medium heat, stirring occasionally, or until soft and lightly golden.

3 Add the garlic, cumin, chilli and cinnamon, and stir-fry for 1 minute.

4 Add all the remaining ingredients and stir to combine. Reduce the heat to low and simmer for 30 minutes.

Preparation time:
15 minutes
Total cooking time:
about 30 minutes
Serves 6

★

¾ cup (130 g/4¼ oz) burghul
2 tablespoons olive oil
1 onion, finely chopped
2 cloves garlic, crushed
2 teaspoons ground cumin
1 teaspoon chilli powder
½ teaspoon ground cinnamon
2 x 410 g (13 oz) cans crushed tomatoes
3 cups (750 ml/24 fl oz) vegetable stock (page 12)
440 g (14 oz) can red kidney beans, drained
440 g (14 oz) can chickpeas, drained
315 g (10 oz) can corn kernels, drained
2 tablespoons tomato paste

133

CORN FRITTERS

Serves 4

1 x 310 g can whole kernel corn
2 eggs
sprinkle of salt and pepper
½ cup plain flour
1 teaspoon baking powder
¼ cup grated cheese
25 g butter
2 tablespoons oil

1 Drain corn. Discard liquid.

2 Put eggs, salt + pepper in a bowl. Beat well.

3 Add flour + baking powder. Whisk until smooth.

4 Add drained corn and grated cheese. Stir.

5 Put butter + oil in frypan. Heat until bubbly. MEDIUM HEAT

6 Drop spoonsful of the mixture in. MEDIUM HEAT

7 When golden, turn over and cook other side.

8 Drain on absorbent paper and serve.

SAVOURY RICE 🍄🍄🍄

Serves 6

1 tablespoon oil
1 onion, chopped
1 x 425 g can peeled tomato pieces (and the juice)
1 teaspoon instant chicken stock powder
sprinkle of salt and pepper
¼ teaspoon sugar
1 x 310 g can whole kernel corn
3½ cups cooked rice
1 cup frozen peas
1 cup grated Cheddar cheese

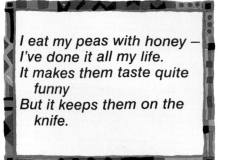

*I eat my peas with honey —
I've done it all my life.
It makes them taste quite funny
But it keeps them on the knife.*

1. Turn oven to 180°C.(350°F) Grease an ovenproof dish.

2. Heat oil in a pan. Add onion. Fry gently.

3. Add tomatoes, stock, salt pepper and sugar.

4. Stir it over low heat for 7 minutes.

5. Drain corn. Mix in a bowl with rice + peas.

6. Spread rice, corn and peas in the dish.

7. Pour tomato mixture over rice.

8. Sprinkle cheese over. Bake for 30 minutes.

RATATOUILLE

1 Heat the oil in a large pan and add the onion. Cook over medium heat, stirring occasionally, for about 10 minutes or until very soft and lightly golden brown.

2 Add the garlic and cook for 1 more minute.

3 Meanwhile, cut the eggplants and zucchinis into slices about 2 cm (³/₄ inch) thick.

4 Remove the seeds and white membrane from the peppers and cut them into 2 cm (³/₄ inch) squares.

5 Add all the vegetables to the pan. Cook, stirring frequently, for about 5 minutes.

6 Reduce the heat to low, cover the pan with a lid and cook for 15 minutes, stirring occasionally.

Preparation time: 20 minutes
Total cooking time: 35 minutes
Serves 6

★

2 tablespoons olive oil
1 large onion, chopped
2 cloves garlic, crushed
3 slender eggplants
(aubergines)
3 medium zucchinis
(courgettes)
1 green pepper (capsicum)
1 red pepper (capsicum)
3 large tomatoes, chopped
⅓ cup (20 g/⅔ oz) chopped
fresh basil

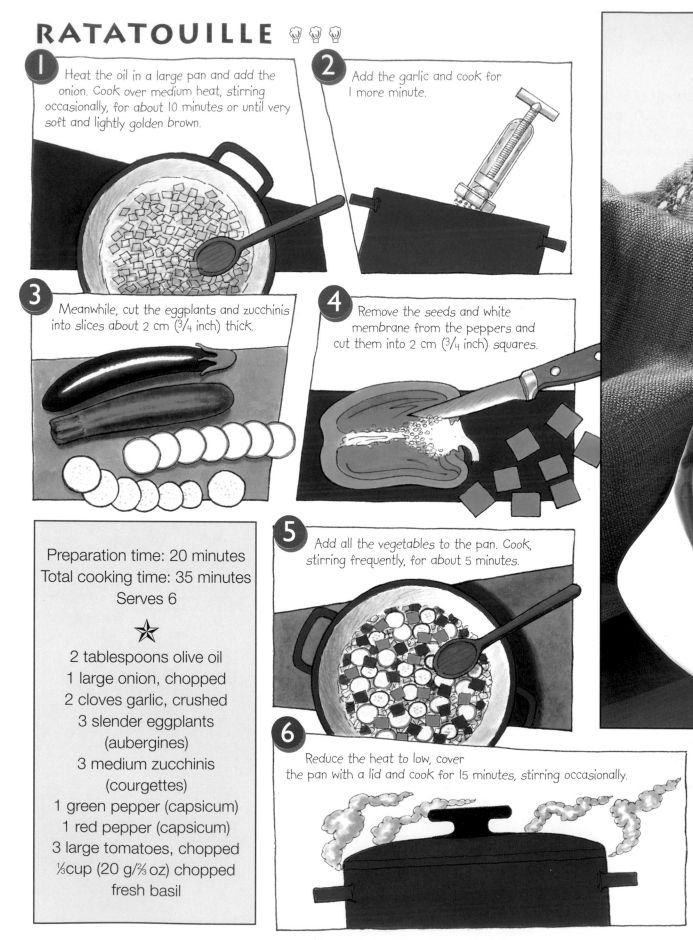

7 Uncover the pan, raise the heat and cook for another 5 minutes to evaporate some of the liquid. Stir in the basil.

NOTE Ratatouille also makes a great pasta sauce. Or it can be used as a filling for tarts if cooked for a further 30 minutes, until almost dry, and then sprinkled with cheese.

BUTTERED CARROTS

Serves 4

4 medium size carrots
30 g butter
1½ teaspoons French
  mustard
1 teaspoon brown sugar
1 tablespoon chopped
  parsley

1
Wash + scrape carrots.
Slice into thin rounds.

2
Put into a flat round
dish.

3
Chop butter. Dot it
over carrots.

4
Stir in the mustard.
Sprinkle sugar over.

5
Cover dish with cling
wrap. Pierce.

6
Cook it on High for
5 minutes.

7
Carefully uncover + stir.
Cover dish again.

8
Cook on High 3½ minutes
Stir in parsley. Serve.

ONION TART

Serves 6

375 g puff pastry
¾ cup grated cheese
50 g butter
2 onions, finely sliced
1 cup evaporated milk
1 tablespoon plain flour
sprinkle of salt and pepper
2 eggs

1

Turn oven to 190°C (375°F).
Roll out the pastry.

2

Line a 24 cm pie dish.
Trim edges neatly.

3

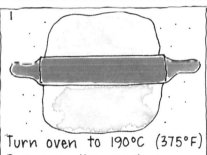

Sprinkle cheese over base.
Put it in the fridge until
the filling is ready.

4

Melt butter in pan.
Gently cook onion until
soft but not brown.

5

Whisk milk, flour, salt,
pepper, eggs in a bowl.

6

Stir in the onions
and the butter.

7

Carefully pour it all
into the pastry base.

8

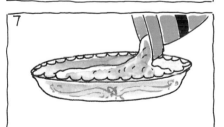

Bake 35-40 minutes
or until it is set.

YUMMY BAKED POTATOES

Potatoes baked or microwaved in their skins or jackets are absolutely delicious. You can eat them hot or cold, just as they are or serve them with a dollop of sour cream or butter. Best of all, scoop out the middle and make one of our delicious recipes.

Baked potatoes are great on their own as a snack or served with a crunchy salad for a light meal. Serve one or two potatoes for each person. A baked potato in your school lunchbox will make a great change from sandwiches.

To make baked potatoes really crispy, brush the skin with a little oil and sprinkle with salt before cooking. To check if potatoes are cooked, hold potato firmly with an oven mitt or dry tea-towel. Push a skewer into the centre of the potato. If it goes in easily, the potato is cooked.

BEFORE YOU COOK

• Don't buy potatoes that look greenish.
• Old potatoes are best for baking.
• Choose potatoes that are about the same size and shape, so they will cook at the same time.
• Scrub potatoes under cold water. Pat dry with paper towels. Do not peel.

HOW TO BAKE POTATOES

Turn oven to 210°C (415°F). Pierce potatoes all over with a fork — this helps potato to cook evenly and to prevent the skin splitting. Place directly on the oven rack. Bake 1 hour or until tender. Remove from oven and cool slightly. Cut potatoes in half with a sharp knife. Scoop out the flesh with a teaspoon, leaving a thin shell. Try not to put a hole in the shell. Use the scooped out potato in the filling.

HOW TO MICROWAVE POTATOES

Pierce potatoes all over with a fork. Wrap each one in a layer of absorbent paper and place directly onto the turntable. For four potatoes, cook on High for 10 minutes. Leave, unopened, for 2 minutes before cutting. Scoop out the flesh with a teaspoon, leaving a thin shell. Try not to put a hole in the shell. Use the scooped out potato in the filling.

Scrub potatoes well. Pierce potatoes all over with a fork.

Place potato directly on oven rack. Bake for 1 hour.

To microwave, pierce potatoes and wrap in absorbent paper. Cook on High.

CHEESY CORN POTATOES

4 medium potatoes
⅔ cup coarsely grated Cheddar cheese
130 g can creamed corn
1 tablespoon chopped chives

1. Turn oven to 210°C (415°F). Pierce potatoes. Place on oven rack. Bake 1 hour OR microwave on High for 10 minutes.
2. Cut potatoes in half, scoop out flesh. Arrange potato shells on oven tray.
3. Mash scooped-out potato in a bowl. Add cheese, corn and chives. Mix well.
4. Spoon filling into shells. Bake 15 minutes OR microwave on Medium 5 minutes. Serve hot.

CRUNCHY TUNA POTATOES

4 medium potatoes
185 g can tuna in oil, drained
¼ cup mayonnaise
1 stick celery, finely chopped
2 tablespoons finely chopped red capsicum
1 tablespoon finely chopped parsley
½ cup breadcrumbs

1. Turn oven to 210°C (415°F). Pierce potatoes. Place on oven rack. Bake 1 hour OR microwave on High for 10 minutes.
2. Cut potatoes in half, scoop out flesh. Arrange potato shells on oven tray.
3. Mash scooped-out potato in a bowl. Add tuna, mayonnaise, celery, capsicum and parsley. Mix well.
4. Spoon filling into shells. Sprinkle with breadcrumbs. Bake 15 minutes OR microwave on Medium for 5 minutes. Serve hot.

BOLOGNESE POTATOES

4 medium potatoes
1 tablespoon oil
125 g minced beef
1 tablespoon tomato paste
¼ cup water
130 g can spaghetti with cheese and tomato sauce
1 spring onion, chopped
2 tablespoons grated Parmesan cheese

1. Turn oven to 210°C (415°F). Pierce potatoes. Place on oven rack. Bake 1 hour OR microwave on High for 10 minutes.
2. Cut potatoes in half, scoop out flesh. Arrange potato shells on oven tray.
3. Heat oil in a small pan. Add mince. Cook 3 minutes until brown. Add tomato paste and water. Stir and bring to the boil.
4. Remove from heat. Stir in spaghetti, onion and cheese.
5. Mash scooped out flesh in a bowl. Mix gently into spaghetti mixture. Spoon filling into shells.
6. Bake 15 minutes OR microwave on Medium for 5 minutes. Serve hot.

When potatoes are cooked, cut in half. Cool slightly.

Scoop out flesh with a spoon. Mix with filling.

Cook mince until all red is gone. Stir to break up lumps.

CHAPTER SIX

DESSERTS AND CAKES

Luscious sweet things to make and enjoy! In this chapter you'll find puddings and cakes, pikelets, trifles, and two types of ice-cream. For a really fun dessert try our White Chocolate Fondue with fresh fruit.

ROCKY ROAD ICE-CREAM 👨‍🍳👨‍🍳

Serves 6

100 g packet red glacé
   cherries
100 g packet coloured
   marshmallows
¼ cup choc bits
¼ cup crushed nuts

2 tablespoons desiccated
   coconut
1 L vanilla ice-cream,
   softened
60 g dark chocolate,
   chopped

This ice-cream makes a great sundae. Fill a long glass with a scoop of rocky road, sliced bananas, more ice-cream and top with chocolate sauce.

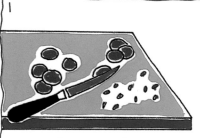

1 Chop cherries finely.

2 Cut marshmallows into pieces.

3 Put cherries, marshmallows choc bits, nuts and coconut in a big bowl.

4 Add ice-cream. Mix gently.

5 Pour into a loaf or bread tin. Smooth the top.

6 Cover with plastic wrap. Put in freezer for 3 hours.

7 Melt dark chocolate in a bowl over hot water.

8 Spoon melted chocolate over ice-cream and serve.

MANGO ICE-CREAM 👨‍🍳👨‍🍳👨‍🍳

Serves 4

2 teaspoons cornflour
2 tablespoons sugar
1 cup cream
1 cup milk
170 g can mango pulp

1 Mix cornflour, sugar and cream in a pan.

2 Add milk. Cook, stirring, until it boils and thickens.

3 Remove from heat. Leave to cool slightly.

4 Stir in mango pulp.

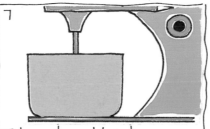

5 Pour mixture into a big plastic bowl. Cover with plastic wrap.

6 Put in freezer 2 hours until the ice-cream hardens a little.

7 Take out and beat on Medium speed 4 minutes.

8 Put in freezer again for 4 hours or until firm.

CHOCOLATE SUNDAE

Serves 4

1 teaspoon cornflour
2 tablespoons cocoa
25 g butter
⅓ cup golden syrup
¼ cup water
4 scoops vanilla ice-cream
chopped walnuts (if liked)

1 Mix cornflour + cocoa powder in a small pan.

2 Add the butter and the golden syrup.

3 Add the water.

4 LOW HEAT
Melt it all together.

5 LOW HEAT
Stir well, simmering gently.

6 Put a scoop of ice-cream into 4 nice dishes.

7 Pour some of the hot sauce over each one.

8 Scatter a few walnuts on top if you like.

CHOCO BANANA SPLIT

Serves 4

¾ cup caster sugar
3 tablespoons cocoa
2 tablespoons water
¾ cup evaporated milk
2 tablespoons butter
½ teaspoon imitation
   vanilla essence
4 medium-sized bananas
4 scoops vanilla ice-cream

1 Put sugar, cocoa, and water in a small pan.

2 Add milk. Stir it until it comes to the boil. LOW HEAT

3 Simmer gently for 5 minutes. Stir in butter and vanilla. LOW HEAT

4 Set it aside to cool for about 10 minutes.

5 Peel, then split the bananas in half.

6 Put 2 halves in each of 4 nice sundae dishes.

7 Put a scoop of ice-cream on top of each.

8 Pour chocolate sauce over each and serve.

FRUIT FLUMMERY 👨‍🍳👨‍🍳

Serves 6
½ cup cold water
1 tablespoon gelatine
¼ cup plain flour
¾ cup caster sugar
½ cup apple juice
1 teaspoon lemon juice
1 cup hot water
the pulp of 4 passionfruit
plain yoghurt, to serve

1

Whisk cold water + gelatine. Set aside.

2

Put flour + sugar in small pan. Add apple juice. Whisk.

3

Add lemon juice + hot water. Whisk.

4

MEDIUM HEAT
Stir over heat until it's thick and bubbly.

5

Take off heat. Add the gelatine. Whisk well.

6

Pour into a bowl. Chill in fridge till it thickens. DON'T let it set!

7
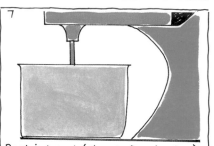
Beat it hard (about 5 minutes) until very thick and pale.

8
Stir in ¾ of the passionfruit pulp. Put into glasses and put in fridge to set.
Serve with yoghurt and the rest of the passionfruit pulp.

CREAMY APRICOT RICE 👨‍🍳👨‍🍳

Serves 4

425 g can apricot halves
540 g can vanilla-flavoured
  rice cream
1 teaspoon grated orange
  rind

1¼ cups thickened cream
2 tablespoons icing sugar
2 tablespoons slivered
  almonds, toasted

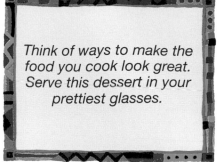

*Think of ways to make the
food you cook look great.
Serve this dessert in your
prettiest glasses.*

1. Drain all the liquid from apricots. Chop half of them.

2. Put chopped apricots + rice cream into a big bowl. Add 1 teaspoon rind. Mix gently.

3. Put cream and sugar in a small bowl. Beat until firm peaks form.

4. Put ½ the cream onto the rice. Mix in the rest of the apricots very gently.

5. Spoon into pretty glasses.

6. Put in fridge for 1 hour.

7. Top with the rest of the cream.

8. Sprinkle with almonds. Serve immediately.

STRAWBERRY BOMBE ALASKA 👨‍🍳👨‍🍳👨‍🍳

Serves 4-6

1 plain sponge cake
4 scoops vanilla ice-cream softened
1 tablespoon strawberry ice-cream topping

2 egg whites
¼ cup caster sugar
1 tablespoon flaked almonds

1 Turn oven to 200°C (400°F). Line a pizza tray with foil.

2 Cut cake in half. Put bottom half on tray.

3 Put ice-cream and topping in a bowl. Mix well.

4 Spoon ice-cream onto middle of cake. (Leave 2cm around edge.)

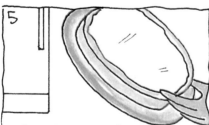

5 Put in freezer for 1 hour or until very firm. Put top on.

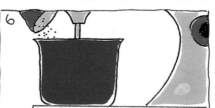

6 Put egg whites in a clean bowl. Beat until stiff, slowly adding sugar.

7 Spread meringue evenly over cake. Sprinkle with almonds.

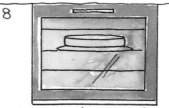

8 Put on centre shelf of oven. Bake for 3-5 minutes. Serve immediately.

WHITE CHOCOLATE FONDUE 👨‍🍳👨‍🍳

Makes 1½ cups
100 g packet white
   marshmallows
125 g white chocolate
½ cup sweetened
   condensed milk
⅓ cup sour cream
1 teaspoon imitation
   vanilla essence
fresh fruit, for dipping

1
Cut marshmallows into small pieces.

2
Chop chocolate coarsely.

3
Put condensed milk in a small pan. Heat gently for 5 minutes.

4
Add marshmallows. Stir until almost smooth.

5
Add chocolate. Take pan off heat.

6
Beat until chocolate melts and sauce is smooth.

7
Add cream and vanilla. Stir gently.

8
To serve, put the sauce in a bowl. Dip fruit in and eat.

CHOC-HONEYCOMB MOUSSE

Serves 4

½ cup thickened cream

250 g milk chocolate, chopped

¼ cup sugar

2 teaspoons gelatine

½ cup water

2 x 35 g chocolate-coated honeycomb bars, chopped

1 Heat cream gently in a small pan.

2 Add chocolate. Take off heat and stir until chocolate melts.

3 Pour into mixing bowl. Put aside to cool.

4 Mix sugar, gelatine and water in a small pan. Stir until sugar dissolves.

5 Turn up heat and boil. Take off heat and pour into mixing bowl.

6 Beat on Medium speed 10 minutes until thick and fluffy.

7 Gently mix chocolate through. Spoon mousse into 4 dishes.

8 Put in fridge for 30 minutes. Sprinkle honeycomb over and serve.

BLUEBERRY PIKELETS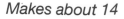

Makes about 14

1 cup self-raising flour
2 tablespoons caster sugar
1 teaspoon grated lemon
   rind
1 egg, lightly beaten
$^1/_3$ cup sour cream
$^1/_2$ cup milk
1 teaspoon oil
1 cup fresh blueberries
$^1/_2$ cup maple syrup

1. Sift flour into a mixing bowl. Stir in sugar and rind.

2. Add egg, cream and milk.

3. Beat until mixture is smooth, with no lumps.

4. Brush a non-stick fry pan with oil. Heat until warm.

5. Drop a tablespoon of batter in. Shape into a circle about 8cm wide.

6. Cook 2 minutes; turn and cook other side 2 minutes until golden.

7. As the pikelets are cooked pile them up on a plate and cover with foil to keep warm.

8. Serve with blueberries piled on. Pour maple syrup over.

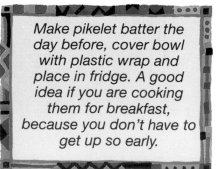
Make pikelet batter the day before, cover bowl with plastic wrap and place in fridge. A good idea if you are cooking them for breakfast, because you don't have to get up so early.

PINEAPPLE CREAM TRIFLE

Serves 6

85 g packet lemon
   jelly crystals
1 cup boiling water
250 g packet jam
   sponge roll
2 tablespoons custard powder

1 cup milk
450 g can crushed
   pineapple, well drained
1¼ cups thickened cream
2 tablespoons icing sugar

> *Trifles are a great way to use up bits and pieces. Any left-over cake will do as the base; use raspberry jelly and tinned peaches for a different flavour.*

1. Put jelly and water in a small bowl. Stir until jelly dissolves.

2. Cut jam roll into slices. Put on bottom of a serving bowl. (About 25 cm.)

3. Pour jelly over cake.

4. Put custard powder and milk in a small pan. Stir until smooth.

5. Cook, stirring slowly, until custard thickens and boils.

6. Take off heat. Stir in pineapple. Put lid on and leave 5 minutes. Spread over jelly.

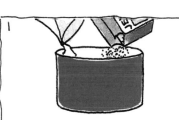

7. Put cream and sugar in a small bowl. Beat until thick. Spread over custard.

8. Cover bowl with plastic wrap. Put in fridge for 2–3 hours.

RASPBERRY ROYAL 👨‍🍳👨‍🍳

Serves 6
85 g strawberry instant
   pudding mix
1 cup milk
2 teaspoons gelatine
1 tablespoon boiling water
300 ml thickened cream,
   whipped
1/2 cup fresh raspberries
250 g packet jam sponge roll

1 Line a medium bowl with plastic wrap.

2 Beat together the pudding mix and milk in a large bowl until smooth.

3 Put the gelatine + boiling water in a small bowl + stir gently until dissolved.

4 Mix gently into the pudding mixture. Add the whipped cream.

5 Add raspberries. Mix gently.

6 Cut cake into 1 cm slices. Cover bottom and sides of serving bowl.

7 Spread raspberry filling on top of cake. Cover with plastic wrap.

Always read the recipe through before you start cooking. Note how long it will take, and work out if you have time to make the dish. Try and plan your cooking well ahead.

8 Put in fridge overnight. Turn out onto a flat plate to serve.

APPLE TURNOVERS 👨‍🍳👨‍🍳

Serves 6

about 200 g puff pastry
2 green apples
2 tablespoons caster sugar
2 teaspoons ground
  cinnamon

1
Turn oven to 190°C (375°F)
Roll pastry out thinly.

2
Cut into 6 squares
14 × 14 cm

3
Peel + core apples. Cut into
quarters. Slice very thinly.

4
Put a few slices of apple
in corner of pastry.

5
Sprinkle apple with a
teaspoon sugar. Add a
pinch of cinnamon.

6
Fold over into neat
triangles. Press edges
with fork to seal well.

7
Prick a hole in top.
Sprinkle a little sugar over.

8
Place on a baking tray.
Bake 20 minutes.

157

BANANA DELICIOUS

Serves 6

4 medium-sized bananas
1 tablespoon lemon juice
2 eggs
2 tablespoons caster sugar
1 cup desiccated coconut
2 tablespoons apricot jam
cream or ice-cream to
    serve

1
Turn oven to 180°C (350°F).
Peel the bananas.

2
Slice the bananas into
an ovenproof dish.

3
Sprinkle the lemon juice
all over.

4
Put eggs + sugar in bowl.
Beat well until creamy.

5
Stir in coconut + jam.
Mix it all well.

6
Pour it all evenly
over the bananas.

7
Bake for 25 minutes or
until golden.

8
Serve warm with cream
or ice-cream.

FRUIT CRUMBLE 👨‍🍳

Serves 6

1 cup canned peach slices
1 cup pineapple pieces
50 g butter
½ cup brown sugar
1 cup bran
1 cup cornflakes
cream or ice-cream, to
   serve

1. Turn oven to 180°C. Drain peaches + pineapples.

2. Put the fruit into an ovenproof dish.

3. Put butter in a pan. Melt on low heat.

4. Take off heat. Stir in brown sugar.

5. Add bran + cornflakes. Stir it well.

6. Sprinkle it evenly over the fruit.

7. Bake for 12-15 minutes.

8. Serve warm with cream or ice-cream.

STEAMED PUDDING 👨‍🍳👨‍🍳👨‍🍳

Serves 6

½ cup strawberry jam
60 g butter
½ cup caster sugar
1 egg

1½ cups plain flour
1 teaspoon baking powder
½ cup milk

1  Grease a 4 cup pudding bowl. Spread jam in the base.	2 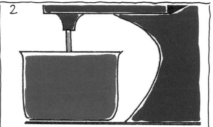 Beat butter, sugar + egg till smooth and creamy.
3  Sift in flour + baking powder. Add milk and mix well.	4 Spread it carefully on top of the jam in bowl.
5 Make a foil lid. Press the edges to seal tight. Make a string handle for it.	6  HIGH HEAT Lower it into big pan with boiling water 5cm deep in it.
7 LOW HEAT Put lid on pan. Turn heat to low. Simmer for 1¼ hours. Keep refilling with water.	8 Run knife round edge of pudding. Tip onto serving plate. Serve.

APPLE PUDDING 👩‍🍳👩‍🍳

Serves 6

5 green apples
¼ cup caster sugar
1 teaspoon grated lemon
    rind
1 tablespoon water
60 g butter
2 tablespoons caster sugar,
    extra
1 egg
½ cup self-raising flour
cream or ice-cream, to
    serve

1  Turn oven to 180°C (350°F) Grease a baking dish.	**2** Peel, core + slice apples. Put in baking dish.	**3** Stir in caster sugar + lemon rind. Add the water.
4  Beat butter, 2 tablespoons sugar + egg till smooth.	**5**  Stir in the flour. Mix well.	**6**  Carefully spread it on top of the apples.
7  Bake it for 30-35 minutes or until golden.	*When you think of the hosts without number Who are slain by the deadly cucumber It's quite a mistake Of such food to partake It results in a permanent slumber.*	**8**  Serve warm with cream or vanilla ice-cream.

BAKED APPLES 👨‍🍳👨‍🍳

Serves 4

4 green apples
½ cup finely chopped dates
1 tablespoon chopped
 walnuts
1 tablespoon grated lemon
 rind
½ cup water
½ cup brown sugar
30 g butter
¼ teaspoon ground
 cinnamon
¼ teaspoon ground nutmeg
ice-cream or whipped
 cream, to serve

1
Turn oven to 180°C (350°F)
Cut core neatly out of apples.

2
Peel the top quarter
off each apple.

3
Mix dates, walnuts + rind well.
Press into centres of apples.

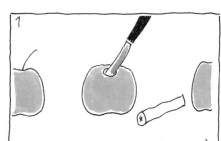
4
Put apples into a pan
or a loaf tin.

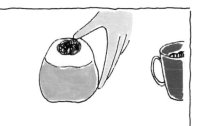
5
Put water, brown sugar, butter,
cinnamon + nutmeg in a pan.

6
Bring it to the boil and
pour it over the apples.

7
Bake them for about 1¼
hours - basting now +
again with the liquid.

There was a young lady
of Ryde
Who ate some green
apples and died.
The apples fermented
Inside the lamented
And made cider inside
her inside.

8
Serve apples hot with
vanilla ice-cream or
whipped cream.

UPSIDE-DOWN CAKE 👨‍🍳👨‍🍳👨‍🍳

Serves 6

125 g butter
¾ cup caster sugar
1 egg
2 cups plain flour
2 teaspoons baking powder
¾ cup milk

1 large banana, mashed
75 g butter, melted
½ cup brown sugar
1 cup well drained crushed
  pineapple
cream, to serve

*'I must leave here,' said
Lady de Vere,
'For these damp airs don't
suit me, I fear.'
Said a lady, 'Dear me!
If they do not agree
With your system, why eat
pears, my dear?*

1 Turn oven to 180°C (350°F)
Have ready a 20 cm
square tin.

2 Beat butter, sugar, egg till
smooth. Sift in flour +
baking powder.

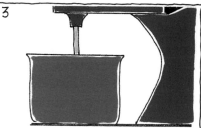
3 Mix it in adding milk and
mashed banana as well.

4 Spread melted butter in
base of the tin.

5 Sprinkle brown sugar
evenly in the base.

6 Carefully spread crushed
pineapple over.

7 Pour batter evenly over.
Bake for 1 hour.

8 Tip out onto plate. Serve
warm with cream.

PANCAKES 👨‍🍳👨‍🍳

Makes about 12

1 cup plain flour
sprinkle of salt
1 egg
1¼ cups milk
a little oil to grease frypan
lemon juice ⎫ to sprinkle
sugar ⎭ over pancakes
cream or ice-cream, to serve

1. Sift flour + salt into mixing bowl. Add egg and milk.

2. NO LUMPS! Whisk + whisk till smooth. Set aside for 1 hour.

3. MEDIUM HEAT
Gently heat a lightly greased 20 cm frypan.

4. Pour batter into a jug for easier pouring.

5. Pour about 3 tablespoons into pan. Tilt pan to spread it all over evenly.

6. Lift edges with a knife. When golden, flip it over and cook the other side.

7. Place on kitchen paper. Sprinkle lemon + sugar over.

8. Roll up and serve hot with whipped cream or ice-cream if you like.

TROPICAL CARROT LOAF 👨‍🍳

Makes one 25 cm loaf
1½ cups grated carrot
225 g can pineapple
    pieces, drained
1 teaspoon grated
    orange rind
2 cups wholemeal
    self-raising flour
¾ cup oil

3 eggs, lightly beaten
⅔ cup caster sugar
1 teaspoon cinnamon
½ teaspoon mixed spice
TOPPING
250 g cream cheese
1 teaspoon grated
    orange rind
½ cup icing sugar

To decorate cake, draw a carrot shape in the icing with a skewer. Carefully fill in the outline with coloured sprinkles.

1
Turn oven to 180°C (350°F). Grease a 25×15cm loaf tin. Line with waxed paper.

2
Put carrot, pineapple, rind, flour, oil, eggs, sugar and spices in a big bowl.

3
Mix well with a fork.

4
Spread evenly in tin. Bake for 55 minutes.

5
Turn cake out and cool on a wire rack.

6
Put cream cheese, rind and icing sugar in a small bowl.

7
Beat until light and fluffy.

8
Turn cake right-side up. Spread topping over cake.

APRICOT LOAF 👩‍🍳👩‍🍳

Makes 1 loaf

½ cup finely chopped dried
   apricots
½ cup milk
125 g butter
½ cup caster sugar

3 eggs
2 cups self-raising flour
1 teaspoon grated lemon
   rind
¼ cup chopped walnuts

*Why is a caterpillar like
hot bread?
Because it's the grub that
makes the butterfly.*

1

Put apricots + milk in a bowl
Set aside for 30 minutes.

2

Turn oven to 180°C (350°F)
Grease 21 × 14cm loaf tin.

3

Beat butter + sugar well
until smooth + creamy.

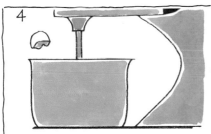

4

Add eggs. Beat them
in very well.

5

Mix in apricots and milk.
Stir in lemon rind.

6

Sift in flour
Mix it in well.

7

Spread it all evenly in
the tin.

8

Sprinkle walnuts on top.
Bake 55–60 minutes.

FUDGE CAKE

Makes 1 x 20 cm cake
1½ cups self-raising flour
3 tablespoons cocoa
1 cup caster sugar
1 cup water
1 teaspoon imitation vanilla
  essence
1 tablespoon white vinegar
½ cup vegetable oil

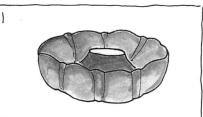

1

Turn oven to 180°C (350°F)
Grease a 20cm fluted
ring tin.

2

Dust the inside of the
tin with a little flour.

3

Put 1¼ cups flour, cocoa,
sugar + water in a bowl.

4

Add vanilla, vinegar and oil.

5

Mix it all together with
a whisk.

6

When smooth, pour it
into the tin.

7

Bake 35-40 minutes. Cool for
10 minutes then take out of tin.

8   ICING
Mix: 1 cup icing sugar
     1½ tablespoons cocoa
     1 tablespoon butter
with a little hot water.
(Use more water if you
want the icing runny.)
Ice the cake.

DOUBLE CHOCOLATE CAKE 👨‍🍳👨‍🍳

Makes one 23 cm cake

125 g butter, softened
¾ cup caster sugar
2 eggs
1¼ cups self-raising flour
2 tablespoons custard powder
⅓ cup cocoa powder
½ cup water
BUTTERCREAM
125 g butter
1⅓ cups icing sugar, sifted
½ cup cocoa powder
2 tablespoons milk

1. Turn oven to 180°C (350°F). Grease a deep 23 cm round cake tin.

2. Put butter, sugar, eggs, flour, custard powder and cocoa in mixing bowl.

3.  Add water. Beat 2 minutes on low speed, then 4 minutes on high speed.

4. Spread evenly in tin. Bake 40 minutes. Turn onto a rack to cool.

5. Put butter, icing sugar, cocoa and milk in a small bowl.

6.  Beat 1 minute on low speed, then 4 minutes on high speed.

7. Cut cake in half. Spread buttercream on bottom half.

Decorate this cake with chocolate buttons, chocolate animals or whatever takes your fancy.

8.  Cover with cake top. Spread buttercream over top and sides.

STICKY HONEY PECAN RING 👨‍🍳👨‍🍳

Makes one 20 cm ring cake

340 g packet buttercake mix
¼ cup sour cream
⅔ cup pecan nuts, finely chopped
⅔ cup honey
1 tablespoon lemon juice
whole pecans, to decorate

1 Turn oven to 180°C (350°F). Grease and line a 20cm ring tin.

2 Follow directions on packet to make cake batter.

3 Add sour cream to batter. Beat well.

4 Add chopped nuts. Mix in gently.

5 Spread evenly in tin. Bake for 45 minutes. Leave to cool for 5 minutes.

6 Put honey and juice in a small pan. Heat until just warm. LOW HEAT

7 Turn cake out onto serving plate. Pour over honey and lemon.

8 Top with nuts. Serve hot.

LEMON BUTTERFLY CAKES 🎩🎩🎩

Makes about 35
340 g packet buttercake
  mix
2 teaspoons grated
  lemon rind
⅔ cup bottled lemon butter
½ cup thickened cream
¼ cup icing sugar
35 silver balls

1 Turn oven to 180°c (350°F). Lay out 35 paper patty cases.

2 Follow directions on packet to make cake batter. Mix in the rind.

3 Put 1 tablespoon batter into each patty case. Bake for 15 minutes. Cool on wire rack.

4 Cut a circle from the top of each cake. Cut circles in half.

5 Put ½ teaspoon lemon butter into each cake.

6 Put cream in a small bowl. Beat until firm peaks form.

7 Put 1 tablespoon cream onto each cake. Press the half-circles on top.

8 Dust with icing sugar. Put a silver ball on top.

CARROT CAKE

Makes 1 x 20 cm cake

1½ cups raw sugar
1 cup oil
4 eggs
3 cups grated carrot
2 cups wholemeal self-
   raising flour
1 teaspoon ground
   cinnamon

1. Turn oven to 180°C (350°F) Grease a 20 cm tin and line base with waxed paper.

2. Put raw sugar + oil in a mixing bowl. Beat well.

3. Add eggs and beat well.

4. Put grated carrot into a large mixing bowl.

5. Sift in wholemeal flour and cinnamon.

6. Pour the egg mixture in. Mix it all well.

7. Pour into tin and bake for 1 hour + 10 minutes.

8. When cold, mix:
   1 cup icing sugar
   1 tablespoon butter
   1 teaspoon lemon rind
   1 teaspoon lemon juice
   with a little hot water to mix

   Spread over cake.

CHOCOLATE CAKE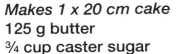

Makes 1 x 20 cm cake
125 g butter
¾ cup caster sugar
2 eggs
1 tablespoon golden syrup
1 teaspoon imitation vanilla essence
1 cup milk
1½ cups self-raising flour
2 tablespoons cocoa

1. Turn oven to 180°C (350°F) Grease a 20cm star-shaped or round tin.

2. Line base of tin with greased waxed paper.

3. Beat butter, sugar + eggs till smooth + creamy.

4. Stir in golden syrup and vanilla.

5. Mix in milk

6. Sift in flour and cocoa. Mix in well.

7. Spread evenly in tin. Bake 45–55 minutes.

8. After 10 minutes take out of tin. Cool completely. Ice with chocolate icing from Fudge Cake.

BANANA CAKE

Makes 1 x 20 cm cake

60 g butter
½ cup caster sugar
1 egg
1 teaspoon imitation vanilla
  essence
1 cup self-raising flour
¼ cup milk
1 ripe banana, mashed
icing, see page 172

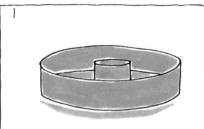

1
Turn oven to 180°C (350°F)
Grease well a 20cm ring tin.

2
Dust all over the inside
of tin with a little flour.

3
Gently melt butter in a
big pan. Don't let it boil.

4
Take off heat and add
sugar, egg + vanilla.

5
Beat it well with a wooden
spoon until smooth.

6
Sift in flour,
Don't stir it yet!

7
Add milk + mashed banana.
Stir until just mixed.

8
Spread evenly in tin. Bake
for 30 minutes. Ice cake
when cold.

BIRTHDAY CAKE 👨‍🍳👨‍🍳

Makes 1 x 20 cm cake

125 g butter
³/₄ cup caster sugar
2 eggs, lightly beaten
1 teaspoon vanilla essence
2 cups self-raising flour
¹/₂ cup milk

1

Turn oven to 180°C. Grease a 20cm round or heart-shaped tin. Line base with waxed paper.

2
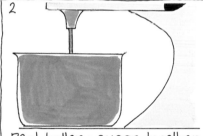
Beat butter + sugar together until smooth + creamy.

3
Add eggs gradually. Beat well each time you add.

4
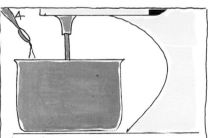
Add the vanilla essence. Beat it all well.

5

Gently fold in alternate spoonfuls of flour and milk until it's all added.

6
Stir until it's smooth. Spread evenly in tin. Bake 40 minutes.

7
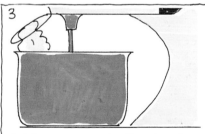
Stick a skewer into the middle of the cake to check it's cooked – the skewer should come out clean.

8

Cool in tin 10 minutes, then turn out + cool completely on wire rack.

Mix 1½ cups icing sugar, 1 tablespoon butter + enough hot water to mix till smooth. Spread over cake. Decorate with jelly beans.

CHAPTER SEVEN

SLICES, COOKIES AND GIFTS

Look through this chapter when you want to make a little something for afternoon tea, when it's time to make a contribution to the local cake stall, or when you just want to make a charming gift for someone special.

VANILLA SLICE 👨‍🍳👨‍🍳

Makes 9
250 g Morning Coffee biscuits
2 cups milk
1 cup cream
85 g packet instant vanilla
   pudding mix
1½ cups icing sugar, sifted
2 tablespoons passionfruit
   pulp
60 g butter, melted

1

Line a deep 19cm square cake tin with foil.

2

Arrange a row of biscuits over the bottom.

3

Put milk and cream in a small mixing bowl. Sprinkle pudding mix on top.

4
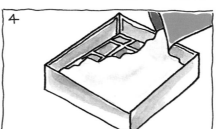
Beat 5 minutes on medium speed. Pour over biscuits.

5

Top with another layer of biscuits (wrong side up).

6

Beat icing sugar, passionfruit and butter in a small bowl until smooth.

7

Spread over biscuits.

8

Put in fridge overnight before cutting. Cut into 9 slices to serve.

CHEESECAKE SLICE 👨‍🍳👨‍🍳👨‍🍳

Makes about 20 slices
85 g packet strawberry
  jelly crystals
1 cup boiling water
60 g butter
125 g dark chocolate,
  chopped
315 g packet plain
  cheesecake mix

1  Line a square cake tin with foil.	2  Put jelly and water in a small bowl. Stir until jelly dissolves.
3  Melt butter gently in a small pan. Add chocolate. Stir until it melts.	4  In a small bowl mix chocolate with biscuit crumbs from cheesecake mix.	5  Press into bottom of tin. Smooth surface.
6  Follow directions on packet to make filling.	7  Spread over biscuit base. Put in fridge for 20 minutes.	8  Top with cooled jelly. Put in fridge 2-3 hours until jelly has set. Cut into squares.

MOCHA WALNUT SLICE 👨‍🍳👨‍🍳

Makes about 16 slices

125 g butter
½ cup milk chocolate melts
3 teaspoons instant coffee
   granules
½ cup caster sugar
1 egg, lightly beaten
1 teaspoon imitation
   vanilla essence
1 cup plain flour
1 cup chopped walnuts

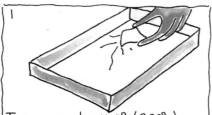

1 Turn oven to 160°c (328°F). Grease a shallow oblong cake tin. Line with baking paper.

2 Melt butter gently in a small pan. Add chocolate. Stir until it melts.

3 Add coffee. Stir until it dissolves.

4 Pour into a big mixing bowl.

5 Add sugar, egg and vanilla. Mix well.

6 Sift flour into bowl. Add walnuts. Mix through gently.

7 Spread evenly in tin. Bake 30 minutes.

Remember to use the timer when you are baking. Don't over-cook this recipe as it is delicious when the middle is still moist and chewy.

8 Cool in tin. Cut into slices to serve.

CHOCOLATE SLICE

Makes about 20 slices
250 g butter
1 cup caster sugar
3 tablespoons cocoa
1 egg, lightly beaten
2 cups desiccated coconut
2 cups cornflakes, crushed
2 cups plain flour
2 teaspoons baking powder
1 teaspoon vanilla essence

1
Turn oven to 180°C (350°F) Lightly grease 30 x 20cm tin.

2
VERY LOW HEAT
Very gently melt the butter in a big pan.

3
Take it off the heat. Whisk in sugar and cocoa.

4
When sugar is dissolved add egg + stir in coconut + cornflakes

5
Stir in flour, baking powder, and vanilla.

6
Stir it all well until it is completely mixed.

7
Press it all firmly into the tin, using your hands.

8
Bake for 20 minutes. When cold ice with chocolate icing, page 91.

BROWNIES

Makes about 20

200 g butter
½ cup cocoa
2 cups brown sugar
1 teaspoon imitation vanilla
essence
1 cup plain flour
2 eggs
½ cup chopped walnuts

1 Turn oven to 180°C
Grease a 30 x 20 cm tin.

2 VERY LOW HEAT
Put butter + cocoa in big pan
Melt gently. Don't boil it!

3 VERY LOW HEAT
Add sugar and vanilla.
Stir it really well.

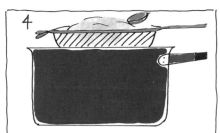

4 Take off heat. Sift in the
flour. Stir it in.

5 Add eggs. Beat them in
really well.

6 Add chopped walnuts.
Stir in.

7 Spread evenly in tin.
Bake 20-25 minutes.

8 When cool, ice with
chocolate icing, see page 91.

LEMON SLICE ♟♟♟

Makes about 14 slices

100 g butter
¼ cup icing sugar
1 cup plain flour

TOPPING
2 eggs
2 tablespoons lemon juice
2 teaspoons grated lemon
  rind
1 cup caster sugar
2 tablespoons plain flour
½ teaspoon baking powder
1 tablespoon icing sugar

1	2	3
Turn oven to 180°C (350°F) Grease a 30 × 20cm tin.	Beat butter and icing sugar until smooth.	Sift in the 1 cup flour. Mix well to a smooth dough.

4	5	6
Press it evenly in the tin. Bake it for 20 minutes. Set aside to cool.	TOPPING: Beat the eggs well. Stir in lemon juice + lemon rind.	Sift in the caster sugar, the 2 tablespoons of flour + baking powder. Stir till mixed.

7	8	
Pour it over the base. Bake again for 25 minutes.	Cool it. ✽ Sift icing sugar on top and cut into squares	*What has one horn and gives milk? A milk truck.*

JAM SLICE 👨‍🍳👨‍🍳

Makes about 24

125 g butter
½ cup caster sugar
1 egg
1½ cups plain flour
1 teaspoon baking powder
½ cup raspberry jam

TOPPING
1 egg
¼ cup caster sugar
1 cup desiccated coconut

1 Turn oven to 180°C. Grease a 20 cm square tin.

2 Put butter in big pan. Melt gently. Take off heat.

3 Add the ½ cup sugar + egg. Whisk it really well.

4 Sift in flour + baking powder. Mix it all well.

5 Spread evenly in tin. Spread jam evenly on top.

6 TOPPING: Put egg, ¼ cup sugar, coconut in bowl. Mix it all well.

7 Sprinkle + spread it evenly over.

8 Bake 30 minutes. Cool it in tin then slice.

COCONUT COOKIES

Makes about 40

125 g butter
³/₄ cup caster sugar
1 egg
1 teaspoon vanilla essence
1 tablespoon white vinegar
1 cup desiccated coconut
2 cups self-raising flour
¹/₂ cup extra coconut

1
Turn oven to 180°C (350°F)
Grease a baking tray.

Beat butter, sugar, egg +
vanilla until smooth.

3
Stir vinegar into bowl.

4
Add coconut.
Sift in flour. Mix well.

5
Roll heaped teaspoonsful
of mixture into balls.

6
Toss each ball in the
extra coconut.

7
Place 5 cm apart on
the baking tray.

8
Bake 15 minutes or till
golden. Cool on wire rack.

ANZAC BISCUITS 👨‍🍳👨‍🍳

Makes about 25

2 cups rolled oats
2 cups plain flour
2 cups desiccated coconut
1½ cups caster sugar
250 g butter
4 tablespoons golden syrup
1 teaspoon baking soda
2 tablespoons boiling water

1 Turn oven to 160°C. Lightly grease oven trays.

2 Put oats, flour, coconut, sugar in big mixing bowl.

3 Melt butter + golden syrup in pan, stirring. Take off heat.

4 Mix baking soda + boiling water in a cup.

5 Add to melted butter in the pan.

6 Quickly add to big bowl. Mix it all well.

7 Roll tablespoonful lots into balls. Put on trays 5 cm apart.

8 Press lightly with fork. Bake 20 minutes — one tray at a time.

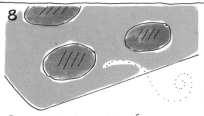

GINGERBREAD PEOPLE 👨‍🍳👨‍🍳👨‍🍳

Preparation time: 1 hour
Total cooking time: about
30 minutes
Makes about 16

★

125 g (4 oz) butter
½ cup (95 g/3¼ oz) lightly packed
soft brown sugar
⅓ cup (115 g/3¾ oz)
golden syrup
1 egg

2 cups (250 g/8 oz) plain flour
⅓ cup (40 g/1⅓ oz) self-raising flour
1 tablespoon ground ginger
1 teaspoon bicarbonate of soda

Icing
1 egg white
1/2 teaspoon lemon juice
1 cup (125 g/4 oz) pure icing
sugar
food colourings

1 Line 2 or 3 oven trays with baking paper. Using electric beaters, beat the butter, sugar and syrup in a bowl until light and creamy. Add the egg and beat well.

2 Transfer the mixture to a large bowl. Sift in the flours, ginger and soda. Use a knife to mix until just combined.

3 Use a well-floured hand to gather the dough into a ball. Knead gently on a well-floured surface until smooth. Don't over-handle the dough or it will become tough.

4 Lay a sheet of baking paper over a large chopping board. Roll out the dough on the lined board to a 5 mm (1/4 inch) thickness. Preheat the oven to moderate 180°C (350°F/Gas 4).

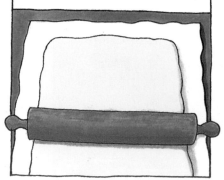

5 Refrigerate the dough on the board for 15 minutes, or until it is firm enough to cut. Cut the dough into shapes using assorted gingerbread people cutters. Press any remaining dough together. Re-roll and cut out into shapes.

6 Bake for 10 minutes or until lightly browned. Cool the biscuits on the trays, then decorate with the icing.

7 To make Icing: Beat the egg white in a small bowl with electric beaters until soft peaks form. Gradually add the lemon juice and sifted icing sugar; and beat until thick and creamy.

8 Divide the icing into several bowls and tint with food colourings.

9 Spoon into small paper icing bags (see page 12) and use to decorate the biscuits.

LEMON COOKIES 👨‍🍳👨‍🍳

Makes about 48

¼ cup milk
1 teaspoon vinegar
125 g butter
¾ cup sugar
1 egg

1 teaspoon grated lemon
 rind
1¾ cups plain flour
1 teaspoon baking powder
¼ teaspoon salt

Customer: May I have a newt-foot sandwich? Sandwich-hand: Sorry, we're out of bread!

1
Turn oven to 180°C (350°F). Mix milk + vinegar in cup. Set aside to turn sour.

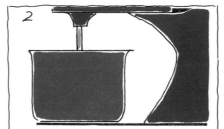
2
Beat butter, sugar, egg + lemon rind until smooth.

3
Sift in flour, baking powder and salt.

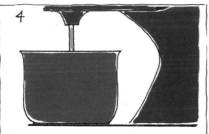
4
Add sour milk. Mix it all together well.

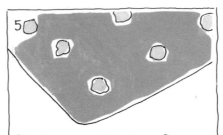
5
Put teaspoonful lots 5cm apart on an oven tray.

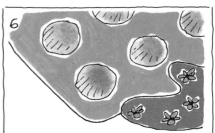
6
Bake 12 minutes or until golden (Bake 1 tray at a time)

7
Lift off tray. Cool on a wire rack. Makes about 48.

8 ●●● Glaze: ●●●●
Mix ½ cup icing sugar + 2 tablespoons lemon juice until mixed + smooth

Spread on hot cookie + ● leave until cold. ●

CHOC-CHERRY SPIDERS 👨‍🍳👨‍🍳

Makes 20

100 g packet glacé cherries

⅓ cup flaked almonds, toasted

100 g packet fried egg noodles

200 g dark chocolate, chopped

30 g butter

1
Chop cherries finely.

2
Put in a bowl with almonds and noodles.

3
Melt chocolate and butter in a small bowl over hot water.

4
Take off heat. Stir until smooth.

5
Add chocolate to cherry mix. Stir gently to combine.

6
Put spoonfuls onto a sheet of greaseproof paper. Leave to set.

7
Dust with icing sugar.

8
Wrap in cellophane and tie with ribbon.

CHERRY MACAROONS

Makes 16

½ cup condensed milk
1 cup desiccated coconut
1 cup shredded coconut
100 g packet glacé cherries
1 tablespoon self-raising
  flour
1 tablespoon custard
  powder

1. Turn oven to 180°c (350°F). Lightly grease 2 biscuit trays.

2. Put condensed milk and all coconut in a mixing bowl.

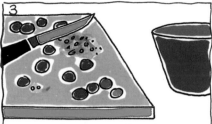
3. Chop cherries finely. Add to bowl.

4. Sift flour and custard powder into bowl.

5. Mix well.

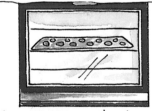
6. Drop tablespoons of mixture onto tray, 4 cm apart.

7. Bake one tray at a time on centre shelf for 15 minutes.

8. Leave on trays 5 minutes. Lift off and cool on wire rack.

CHUNKY CHOCOLATE COOKIES

Makes 16
½ cup brown sugar
1 egg
⅓ cup oil
2 tablespoons cocoa powder
½ cup self-raising flour
½ cup plain flour
⅓ cup choc bits
60 g white chocolate,
    chopped

1. Turn oven to 180°c (350°F). Lightly grease 2 biscuit trays.

2. Put sugar, egg and oil in a mixing bowl. Mix well with a fork.

3. Sift cocoa and flours into bowl.

4. Add chocolates. Mix through gently.

5. Knead lightly with hands to make a soft dough.

6. Make balls by rolling 1 tablespoon of dough.

7. Put balls on tray 4cm apart. Bake 1 tray at a time for 12 minutes.

8. Leave on tray 5 minutes, then cool on wire rack.

CUTOUT CHRISTMAS COOKIES 👨‍🍳👨‍🍳

Makes 12-14 biscuits

125 g butter
⅔ cup icing sugar
1 egg yolk
2 teaspoons imitation
   vanilla essence

2 cups plain flour
1 tablespoon currants

1
Turn oven to 160°c (325°F).

2
Put butter, sugar, egg yolk and vanilla in a small bowl. Beat until light and creamy.

3
Sift flour into bowl. Add currants. Mix to a soft dough.

4
Knead gently on a lightly-floured board. Divide in half.

5
Roll out half the pastry between sheets of baking paper.

6
Roll out thinly. Repeat with other half of pastry. Put in fridge for 20 minutes.

7
Cut dough into shapes. Bake on top shelf for 20 minutes.

Leave on trays 5 minutes. Lift off and cool on wire rack.

COCONUT MARSHMALLOWS

Makes 16

1 cup sugar
1 tablespoon gelatine
¾ cup hot water
½ teaspoon coconut essence
1 cup desiccated coconut

1 Line a deep 19 cm square cake tin with foil.

2 Put sugar, gelatine and water in a small pan. Stir 5 minutes.

3 Simmer 5 minutes more without stirring.

4 Turn up heat. Boil without stirring for 5 minutes more.

5 Take pan off heat. Leave for 5 minutes, then beat for 5 minutes. Stir in essence.

6 Spread marshmallow evenly in tin. Leave for 1 hour until firm.

7 Put coconut in pan. Heat gently until golden. Take off heat and cool.

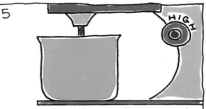

8 Cut marshmallow in squares and toss in coconut. Wrap brightly.

BANANA BITES

Makes about 10

2 medium bananas
125 g milk chocolate melts
1 teaspoon oil
½ cup chocolate sprinkles

1 Peel bananas. Cut off ends.

2 Cut into 3cm slices.

3 Melt chocolate in a bowl over hot water.

4 Take off heat. Add oil. Stir until smooth.

5 Spread sprinkles on a sheet of greaseproof paper.

6 Using a skewer, dip banana into chocolate.

7 Roll banana in sprinkles.

8 Stand on greaseproof paper. Leave to set at room temperature.

197

CHOCOLATE TRUFFLES 👩‍🍳👩‍🍳👩‍🍳

1 Combine the butter and cream in a small pan. Stir over low heat until the butter has melted. Bring to the boil and remove from the heat immediately.

2 Place the chopped chocolate in a heatproof bowl and pour in the hot cream mixture. Cover the bowl for about 1 minute and then stir until the chocolate has melted and the mixture is completely smooth.

3 If adding liqueur or flavourings (see note), stir them in at this stage. Cool the mixture completely in the refrigerator.

4 When the mixture is firm enough to handle, roll heaped teaspoons into balls.

5 Roll the balls in the grated chocolate. Place the truffles on a foil-lined tray and refrigerate until completely firm. These are delicious served with coffee. They will keep in an airtight container for at least 3 weeks.

NOTE Add 1–2 tablespoons of your favourite liqueur to flavour the truffles. If you prefer not to use alcohol, add 1–2 teaspoons of any essence; for example, rum, strawberry or orange.
The truffles can be rolled in cocoa powder or drinking chocolate instead of the grated chocolate.

Preparation time:
40 minutes + refrigeration
Total cooking time:
4 minutes
Makes about 24

⭐

50 g (1⅔oz) butter
⅓cup (80 ml/2¾fl oz) cream
250 g (8 oz) dark chocolate, chopped
100 g (3⅓oz) dark, milk or white chocolate, grated

CRISPY APRICOT BALLS 👨‍🍳👨‍🍳

Makes 24 balls

⅔ cup crushed plain
   biscuit crumbs
1 cup Rice Bubbles
⅓ cup desiccated coconut
250 g white chocolate,
   chopped

1 tablespoon oil
3 tablespoons apricot
   jam
⅔ cup coloured sprinkles

Roll these balls in crushed
nuts or desiccated
coconut instead of
sprinkles if you like.

1 Put biscuit crumbs, Rice
Bubbles and coconut in
bowl. Mix gently.

2 Melt chocolate in a bowl
over hot water.

3 Take off heat. Add oil.
Stir until smooth.

4 Put jam in a small pan.
Warm gently — don't let
it boil.

5 Make a well in centre
of crumb mixture.

6 Pour in melted chocolate
and jam. Mix gently.

7 Make balls by rolling 1
tablespoon of mixture.

8 Roll balls in sprinkles.
Leave to set at room
temperature.

PECAN TARTS 👨‍🍳👨‍🍳

Makes 8

8 frozen shortcrust
   pastry cases
¼ cup self-raising flour
½ teaspoon mixed spice
⅔ cup chopped pecan nuts
1 egg, lightly beaten
1 tablespoon milk
2 tablespoon golden syrup
½ teaspoon imitation
   vanilla essence

1  Turn oven to 190°C (375°F). Arrange tart cases on an oven tray.	**2** Sift flour and spice into a mixing bowl.	**3** Add nuts. Stir to mix. Make a well in the centre.
4 Add egg, milk, golden syrup and vanilla.	**5**  Beat with a fork until almost smooth.	**6**  Spoon filling evenly into tarts.
7 Bake on top shelf 15 minutes. Cool on a rack.	**8**  Put in little boxes, wrap in cellophane and tie with ribbon.	 *Pecans are full of vitamins. North American Indians carried roasted pecans with them on hunting trips as emergency rations.*

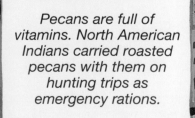

PATTY CAKES 👨‍🍳👨‍🍳

Makes about 30

2 cups self-raising flour
¾ cup sugar
125 g soft butter
3 eggs
½ cup milk
½ teaspoon vanilla
    essence

1
Turn oven to 180°C (350°F)
Set out 30 paper patty cases

2
Sift flour, sugar into
mixing bowl.

3
Add butter, eggs, milk
and vanilla.

4
Beat it all very fast
until it's quite smooth.

5
Fill patty cases until
¾ full with the mixture.

6
Bake for 15 minutes
until golden.

7
Cool on a wire rack
and then ice them.

8 ●● ICING ●●●●●●
Mix: ¾ cup icing sugar
1 teaspoon cocoa or
2-3 drops pink food
colouring
1 tablespoon butter
With: a little hot water
until quite smooth.
Ice the cakes. ●●●

GIFTS FROM THE KITCHEN

You can make some really scrumptious gifts in your own kitchen — it's easy and it's fun. We have given you recipes for Fudge, Coconut Ice and Rum Truffles but you can also make gifts of any of the baked cakes, cookies and slices in the other chapters. Whenever a family birthday, celebration or Christmas comes around you can simply choose any of these favourite sweets or baked goodies to make and wrap.

Do take care when making any of the sweets as the mixtures that need cooking can become very hot.

To dress up your packages use clear or coloured cellophane, tissue paper, printed paper (or paint your own), small cardboard boxes, baskets or pretty tins. You'll also need brightly coloured ribbon and curling tape. Make your own labels from plain paper or cardboard and paint flowers or patterns and the person's name on them.

SOFT FUDGE

125 g plain milk chocolate
50 g butter
¼ cup evaporated milk
3 cups icing sugar

1 Lightly grease a 20 cm square tin.
2 Break up chocolate. Put in top of double boiler.
3 Add butter. Melt it all over gently simmering water.
4 Take it off the heat. Stir in evaporated milk
5 Sift in icing sugar. Mix it all well.
6 Press it all evenly into the tin.
7 Put in fridge until set.
8 Cut it into little squares.

Take melted chocolate and butter off heat, stir in evaporated milk.

Sift in the icing sugar and stir well to mix evenly.

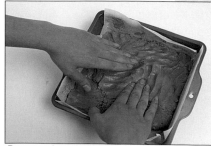

Press mixture evenly over the base of a square cake tin.

202

COCONUT ICE

2 cups icing sugar
3¹/₂ cups desiccated coconut
400 g can condensed milk
2-3 drops red food colouring

Add the condensed milk.

Knead until the colour is even.

Cut into squares.

1 Lightly grease a 20 cm square cake tin. Line with baking paper.
2 Sift icing sugar into a large bowl, add half the coconut. Make a well in the centre and add the condensed milk.
3 Stir with a wooden spoon, then add remaining coconut and mix it in with your hands.
4 Put half the mixture into another bowl, add food colouring and knead until the colour is even.
5 Press the pink mixture into the prepared tin, then press the white mixture on top. Smooth with the back of a spoon.
6 Put the tin into the refrigerator for 1 hour, until mixture has set. Cut into small squares to serve.

RUM TRUFFLES

1 cup cake crumbs
3 tablespoons caster sugar
70 g ground almonds
1 teaspoon cocoa
2 tablespoons grated chocolate
1 egg yolk
1 tablespoon rum
70 g packet chocolate hail
20 foil or paper sweet cases

1 Put crumbs, caster sugar and ground almonds in bowl.
2 Add cocoa, chocolate, egg yolk and rum.
3 Mix it well until it forms quite a smooth paste.
4 Divide it up into small tea-spoonful lots.
5 Roll in cool, dry hands to form a ball.
6 Roll each ball in chocolate hail until covered.
7 Place each truffle in a foil or paper sweet case.
8 Put in a covered container in fridge until firm. They keep in fridge for about 10 days.

Divide rum truffle mixture evenly into small teaspoonfuls.

Roll each teaspoonful into small balls.

Roll each ball in chocolate hail until well covered.

INDEX

A

Anzac biscuits, 187
apples:
Apple muffins, 33
Apple pudding, 162
Apple turnovers, 157
Baked apples, 163
apricots:
Apricot loaf, 167
Apricot-studded pudding, 110
Creamy apricot rice, 149
Crispy apricot balls, 199
Easy apricot chicken, 101
Lamb and apricot parcels, 78
Asian beef and vegetables, 76

B

Baked apples, 163
bananas:
Banana cake, 174
Banana bites, 197
Banana delicious, 158
Banana milkshake, 39
Butterscotch bananas, 112
Choco banana split, 147
beans:
Bean salad, 122
Hot bean dogs, 20
Sausage and bean
bake, 71
beef:
Asian beef and
vegetables, 76
Beef casserole, 74
Beef stroganoff, 103
Crispy Tex-Mex
casserole, 73
Hamburger with the
lot, 75
Hearty beef pie, 69
Macaroni mince, 50
Meat loaf, 77
Mince 'n' mushroom
pizza, 57
Mini mince cups, 104
Savoury pie, 68
Sweet and sour
meatballs, 72
Big pizza, 52
Birthday cake, 175
biscuits see cookies
B.L.T, 29

Blueberry pikelets, 154
bread: see also buns, toast
Ham and cheese
bread, 94
Garlic bread, 95
Gingerbread people, 188
Brownies, 182
buns:
Pizza snacks, 22
Microwave buns, 117
Sticky buns, 31
burgers:
Chicken fillet burgers, 60
Hamburger with the
lot, 75
Buttered carrots, 138
Butterscotch bananas, 112

C

Cabbage bake, 109
cakes:
Apricot loaf, 167
Banana cake, 174
Birthday cake, 175
Carrot cake, 172
Chocolate cake, 173
Double chocolate cake 169
Fudge cake, 168
Hazlenut fudge cake, 115
Lemon butterfly cakes, 171
Microwave buns, 117
Patty cakes, 201
Pineapple cake, 116
Sticky buns, 31
Sticky honey pecan
ring, 170
Tropical carrot loaf, 166
Upside-down cake, 164
cannelloni:
Corny chicken
cannelloni, 47
carrots:
Buttered carrots, 138
Carrot cake, 172
Golden carrot
puddings, 114
Tropical carrot loaf, 166
cheese:
Cheese and potato
bake, 108
Cheese snack, 97
Cheese toast, 14
Cheesy sausage
slice, 96

Ham and cheese
bread, 94
Ham and cheese
puffs, 30
Macaroni cheese, 48
Pizza snacks, 22
Sunken submarines, 26
Cheesecake slice, 179
cherries:
Cherry-berry spider, 36
Cherry macaroons, 192
Choc-cherry spiders, 191
chicken:
Chicken and corn
soup, 93
Chicken and ginger, 65
Chicken and
vegetables, 66
Chicken club sandwich, 28
Chicken fillet burgers, 60
Chicken noodle
omelette, 25
Chicken pockets, 27
Chicken satay, 62
Chicken wings, 64
Chinese lemon chicken, 63
Corny chicken
cannelloni, 47
Creamy chicken, 98
Crispy chicken rolls, 61
Easy apricot chicken, 101
Grilled chicken, 67
Microwave wings, 99
Choco banana split, 147
chocolate:
Brownies, 182
Choc-cherry spiders, 191
Choc-honeycomb
mousse, 153
Choc-mint dream, 36
Choco banana split, 147
Chocolate cake, 173
Chocolate crunch, 118
Chocolate fudge sauce, 111
Chocolate slice, 181
Chocolate sundae, 146
Chocolate truffles, 198
Choconana muffins, 32
Chunky chocolate
cookies, 193
Double chocolate cake, 169
Icing, 168
Spiky crackles, 119
White choclate fondue, 152
Christmas cookies, 194

Cinnamon toast, 15
coconut:
    Coconut cookies, 186
    Coconut ice, 203
    Coconut marshmallows, 196
Coffee float, 38
Coleslaw, 124
cookies:
    Anzac biscuits, 187
    Cherry macaroons, 192
    Chunky chocolate
        cookies, 193
    Coconut cookies, 186
    Cutout Christmas
        cookies, 194
    Lemon cookies, 190
corn:
    Chicken and corn soup, 93
    Corn fritters, 134
    Corny chicken
        cannelloni, 47
Combination noodles, 51
cornflakes:
    Chocolate crunch, 118
    Fruit crumble, 159
Corny chicken cannelloni, 47
Creamy apricot rice, 149
Creamy chicken, 98
Crispy apricot balls, 199
Crispy chicken rolls, 61
Crispy Tex-Mex casserole, 73
curry:
    Spicy lamb curry, 102
Cutout Christmas cookies, 194

D

drinks:
    Banana milkshake, 39
    Cherry-berry spider, 36
    Choc-mint dream, 36
    Coffee float, 38
    Energy shake, 37
    Fruit punch, 41
    Fruit salad smoothie, 37
    Lemon cordial, 40
    Melty malted smoothie, 37
    Pina colada smoothie, 37
Double chocolate cake, 169

EF

Easy apricot chicken, 101
eggs:
    Pavlova roll, 113
    Spanish omelette, 106
Energy shake, 37
Fabulous fettuccine, 44
Fancy fish fingers, 86
fish:
    Fancy fish fingers, 86
    Fish cakes, 84
    Fried seafood rice, 87
    Salmon mornay, 88
    Salmon pasta pots, 83
    Tasty tuna triangles, 18
    Tuna and macaroni
        bake, 46
    Tuna loaf, 89
Freckle faces, 34
French vegetables, 105
Fried seafood rice, 87
fruit:
    Fruit crumble, 159
    Fruit flummery, 148
    Fruit punch, 41
    Fruit salad smoothie, 37
Fruity yoghurt pops, 35
fudge:
    Fudge cake, 168
    Soft fudge, 202

G

Garlic bread, 95
Garlic toast, 16
ginger:
    Chicken and ginger, 65
    Gingerbread people, 188
Glazed pumpkin, 130
Greek salad, 128
green beans:
    Bean salad, 122
Grilled chicken, 67
Golden carrot
    puddings, 114

HI

ham:
    Ham and cheese
        bread, 94
    Ham and cheese
        puffs, 30
    Ham and pineapple, 82
    Pea and ham soup, 92
    Sunken submarines, 26
Hazlenut fudge cake, 115
Hearty beef pie, 69
Hot bean dogs, 20

ice-cream:
    Choco-banana split, 147
    Chocolate sundae, 146
    Coffee float, 38
    Mango ice-cream, 145
    Rocky road
        ice-cream, 144
icing:
    Chocolate, 168
    Lemon, 172

JKL

Jam slice, 184
kidney beans:
    Bean salad, 122
lamb:
    Lamb and apricot
        parcels, 78
    Lamb hot pot, 80
    Lamb kebabs, 79
    Spicy lamb curry, 102
lemons:
    Icing, 172
    Lemon butterfly cakes, 171
    Lemon cookies, 190
    Lemon cordial, 40
    Lemon slice, 183

M

macaroni:
    Macaroni cheese, 48
    Macaroni mince, 50
Mango ice-cream, 145
mayonnaise:
    Potato salad, 123
Meat loaf, 77
Meaty pizza wedges, 54
Melty malted
    smoothie, 37
Mexican pizza, 53
Microwave buns, 117
Microwave wings, 99
milk:
    Banana milkshake, 39
    Coffee float, 38
Mince 'n' mushroom
    pizza, 57
Mini mince cups, 104
Mixed salad, 126
Mocha walnut slice, 180
muffins:
    Apple muffins, 33
    Choconana muffins, 32

NO

Nachos, 19
omelette:
Chicken noodle omelette, 25
Spanish omelette, 106
onions:
Onion and tomato, 131
Onion dip, 17
Onion tart, 139
oranges:
Fruit punch, 41
Oven fries, 132

P

Pancakes, 165
pasta:
Corny chicken cannelloni, 47
Fabulous fettuccine, 44
Macaroni cheese, 48
Macaroni mince, 50
Spaghetti bolognese, 45
Tuna and macaroni bake, 46
pastry:
Apple turnovers, 157
Ham and cheese puffs, 30
Onion tart, 139
Sausage pie, 70
Savoury puff pinwheels, 21
Patty cakes, 201
Pavlova roll, 113
Pea and ham soup, 92
peaches:
Fruit crumble, 159
Pecan tarts, 200
pies:
Hearty beef pie, 69
Sausage pie, 70
Savoury pie, 68
Pina colada smoothie, 37
pineapple:
Fruit crumble, 159
Ham and pineapple, 82
Pineapple cake, 116
Pineapple cream trifle, 155
Pineapple pan pizza, 55
pizza:
Big pizza, 52
Meaty pizza wedges, 54
Mexican pizza, 53
Mince 'n' mushroom pizza, 57
Pineapple pan pizza, 55
Pizza snacks, 22

Pizza supreme, 56
pork:
Ham and pineapple, 82
Schnitzel sandwich, 24
Spareribs in plum
sauce, 81
potatoes:
Cheese and potato
bake, 108
Oven fries, 132
Potato salad, 123
Scalloped potatoes, 129
Yummy baked potatoes, 140
puddings:
Apple pudding, 162
Apricot-studded
pudding, 110
Golden carrot puddings, 114
Steamed pudding, 160
pumpkin:
Glazed pumpkin, 130
punch:
Fruit punch, 41

R

Raspberry royale, 156
Ratatouille, 136
rice:
Creamy apricot rice, 149
Fried seafood rice, 87
Savoury rice, 135
Savoury rice ring, 100
Rocky road ice-cream, 144
Rum truffles, 203

S

salads:
Bean salad, 122
Coleslaw, 124
Greek salad, 128
Mixed salad, 126
Potato salad, 123
Tomato salad, 125
Salmon mornay, 88
Salmon pasta pots, 83
sausages:
Cheesy sausage slice, 96
Sausage and bean bake, 71
Sausage pie, 70
Savoury pie, 68
Savoury puff pinwheels, 21
Savoury rice, 135
Savoury rice ring, 100

Scalloped potatoes, 129
Schnitzel sandwich, 24
slices:
Cheesecake slice, 179
Chocolate slice, 181
Jam slice, 184
Lemon slice, 183
Mocha walnut slice, 180
Vanilla slice, 178
Soft fudge, 202
soup:
Chicken and corn, 93
Pea and ham, 92
Spareribs in plum sauce, 81
Spanish omelette, 106
Spaghetti bolognese, 45
Spicy lamb curry, 102
Spiky crackles, 119
Sticky buns, 31
Sticky honey pecan ring, 170
Strawberry bombe Alaska, 150
Steamed pudding, 160
Sunken submarines, 26
Sweet and sour meatballs, 72

T

Tasty tuna triangles, 18
tarts:
Onion tart, 139
Pecan tarts, 200
toast:
Cheese toast, 14
Cinnamon toast, 15
Garlic toast, 16
tomatoes:
Onion and tomato, 131
Tomato salad, 125
trifle:
Pineapple cream trifle, 155
Tropical carrot loaf, 166
truffles:
Chocolate truffles, 198
Rum truffles, 203
tuna:
Tasty tuna triangles, 18
Tuna and macaroni bake, 46
Tuna loaf, 89

UVW

Upside-down cake, 164
Vanilla slice, 178
Vegetarian chilli, 133
White chocolate fondue, 152

USEFUL INFORMATION

The recipes in this book are all thoroughly tested,
using standard metric measuring cups and spoons.
All cup and spoon measurements are level.
We have used eggs with an average weight of 60 g each
in all recipes.

WEIGHTS AND MEASURES

In this book, metric measures and their imperial equivalents have been rounded out to the nearest figure that is easy to use. Different charts from different authorities vary slightly; the following are the measures we have used consistently throughout our recipes.

OVEN TEMPERATURE CHART

	°C	°F
Very slow	120	250
Slow	150	300
Mod. slow	160	325
Moderate	180	350
Mod hot	210 (190 gas)	425
Hot	240 (200 gas)	475
Very hot	260 (230 gas)	525

LENGTH

Metric	Imperial
5 mm	¼ in
1 cm	½ in
2 cm	¾ in
2½ cm	1 in
5 cm	2 in
8 cm	3 in
10 cm	4 in
12 cm	5 in
15 cm	6 in
20 cm	8 in
25 cm	10 in
30 cm	12 in
46 cm	18 in
50 cm	20 in
61 cm	24 in

CUP AND SPOON MEASURES

A basic metric cup set consists of 1 cup, ½ cup, ⅓ cup and ¼ cup sizes.

The basic spoon set comprises 1 tablespoon, 1 teaspoon, ½ teaspoon and ¼ teaspoon.

1 cup	250 ml (8 fl oz)
½ cup	125 ml (4 fl oz)
⅓ cup (4 tablespoons)	80 ml (2½ fl oz)
¼ cup (3 tablespoons)	60 ml (2 fl oz)
1 tablespoon	20 ml
1 teaspoon	5 ml
½ teaspoon	2.5 ml
¼ teaspoon	1.25 ml

LIQUIDS

Metric	Imperial
30 ml	1 fl oz
60 ml	2 fl oz
100 ml	3½ fl oz
125 ml	4 fl oz (½ cup)
155 ml	5 fl oz
170 ml	5½ fl oz (⅔ cup)
200 ml	6½ fl oz
250 ml	8 fl oz (1 cup)
300 ml	9½ fl oz
375 ml	12 fl oz
410 ml	13 fl oz
470 ml	15 fl oz
500 ml	16 fl oz (2 cups)
600 ml	1 pt (20 fl oz)
750 ml	1 pt 5 fl oz (3 cups)
1 litre (1000 ml)	1 pt 12 fl oz (4 cups)

DRY INGREDIENTS

Metric	Imperial
15 g	½ oz
30 g	1 oz
45 g	1½ oz
60 g	2 oz
75 g	2½ oz
100 g	3½ oz
125 g	4 oz
155 g	5 oz
185 g	6 oz
200 g	6½ oz
250 g	8 oz
300 g	9½ oz
350 g	11 oz
375 g	12 oz
400 g	12½ oz
425 g	13½ oz
440 g	14 oz
470 g	15 oz
500 g	1 lb (16 oz)
750 g	1 lb 8 oz
1 kg (1000 g)	2 lb

GLOSSARY

capsicum = sweet pepper
cornflour = cornstarch
flour = use plain all purpose
    unless otherwise
    specified
eggplant = aubergine
spring onion = shallot
zucchini = courgettes

First published 2003 by Murdoch Books Ltd,
Ferry House, 51–57 Lacy Road, Putney,
London SW15 1PR, UK.
This edition published 2003 for Index Books Ltd,
Henson Way, Kettering, NN16 8PX, UK

ISBN 1 740453 18 2
A catalogue record for this book is available from the British library

Managing Editor: Anna Cheifetz

Design Manager: Helen Taylor

Chief Executive: Juliet Rogers

Production Manager: James Mills-Hicks

Colour separation by Colourscan, Singapore

Printed in Slovenia